EMERGENCY QUESTIONS

RICHARD HERRING

EMERGENCY QUESTIONS

1001
CONVERSATION SAVERS FOR EVERY OCCASION

sphere

SPHERE

First published in Great Britain in 2018 by Sphere
This paperback edition published in 2019 by Sphere

3 5 7 9 10 8 6 4

A CIP catalogue record for this book
is available from the British Library.

ISBN 978-0-7515-7438-8

Typeset in Bembo by M Rules
Printed and bound in Great Britain by
Clays Ltd, Elcograf S.p.A.

Papers used by Sphere are from well-managed forests
and other responsible sources.

Sphere
An imprint of
Little, Brown Book Group
Carmelite House
50 Victoria Embankment
London EC4Y 0DZ

An Hachette UK Company
www.hachette.co.uk

www.littlebrown.co.uk

To Chris Evans (not that one)
(or that one)

CONTENTS

EMERGENCY QUESTIONS

INTRODUCTION

Welcome to the wonderful, bewildering and hilarious world of *Emergency Questions* – a thousand and one questions designed to turn awkward silences into (occasionally) awkward conversations. You can use them at parties, on dates, with strangers on public transport or to find out stuff you never knew about your closest friends.

Some Emergency Questions are outrageous, some crude, some surreal, some mundane. Many are just plain childish and silly, but they're not just thrown together (well not entirely) – they're designed to create stories, often ones that even the person telling them won't have thought to tell before. See them as a starting point for a dialogue. Some of them you will have answers for straight away, some will require a bit of thought and chat and clarification, but if one doesn't work for you then there are plenty more to move on to.

Emergency Questions originated in my internet interview show, *Richard Herring's Leicester Square Theatre*

Podcast (the cool kids have started calling it *RHLSTP*). I didn't want to ask my comedian guests the kind of questions that they have always been asked in interviews, partly because I've been interviewed myself and know how boring that becomes, but mainly because if you've answered the same questions many times your brain flicks to a well-rehearsed script. I wanted to hear stories that hadn't been told before, but also to have some go-to questions if I found myself with nothing to say.

Aren't those the two main concerns of any conversation?

I found that once my guests were in improvisational mode, they became a lot more open and relaxed, and revealed secrets or extra details about things that they had discussed before. Not only did this lead to some wonderful indiscretions, but also some serious revelations – most famously Stephen Fry feeling comfortable enough to discuss a recent suicide attempt.

People have also told me they have used the questions to help them through all kinds of stressful circumstances, and they have even been used as a teaching aid in a South Korean school, with nine year olds being asked to write an essay about whether they would prefer a ham hand or a suncream armpit and the relative benefits of each.

Mostly, though, these questions lead to hilarity. I love it when a guest and I riff through all the possibilities of the more surreal scenarios. David Mitchell is particularly adept at asking qualifying questions, and ultimately that's what this book is all about: generating the kind of fun that comes from chatting and laughing with friends and people that you hope will be friends. The more we talk, the more we learn about each other, and that's nearly always a good thing ... except maybe with the human centipede question.

SOME SUGGESTIONS ON HOW TO ENSURE THIS BOOK IS FUN

KNOW YOUR AUDIENCE

Some of these questions are not suitable for all audiences. Please consider this and ignore or adapt if necessary. You know your audience better than I do, and asking a distant relative about their preferred partners in a human centipede whilst at a funeral might be a mistake. On the other hand, it might be just the icebreaker you need.

NOT ALWAYS SUITABLE FOR MINORS

Kids love these questions, but some of them are not suitable. There is a section of 101 questions for kids, but many others will work too. Just be careful. And change some nouns and verbs here and there.

DON'T FEAR BRAIN FREEZE

Some of the questions are unlikely to lead to a story for everyone and are designed to put you in a hole that you then have to get out of. Maybe your friend has never been in a canoe, or it's possible they've never seen a Bigfoot. Try digging deeper! Use these queries as a springboard to a different conversation: maybe your friend *has* been in a coracle or seen Bigfoot-based comedy film *Harry and the Hendersons*, and you can then talk about that. Hold your nerve.

EGGY DEAD ENDS

It doesn't matter if a question leads to an eggy dead end, because Emergency Questions are about getting out of eggy dead ends. Just ask the next question and hope that it gets you out of your conversational quagmire ... or discuss other times you've been in eggy dead ends.

EMBRACE THE AMBIGUITY

Many of the questions are deliberately ambiguous. You will have a lot of fun if you interpret them in different ways than the one that is immediately apparent.

LISTEN

The point of asking questions is to hear the answers. If you hear something that piques your interest, then ask your own follow-up questions and answer their questions too. This book is at its best when you no longer need the book.

THERE ARE NO CORRECT ANSWERS

In fact, the less correct the better. Have fun and learn some stuff about each other that you might have been better off never knowing!

MOST IMPORTANT: DO NOT SEND ME YOUR OWN EMERGENCY QUESTIONS

All your ones are rubbish (though kids can sometimes come up with good ones). It takes real skill to come up with a question like: Have you ever flown a kite? Don't be so arrogant as to think that you can compete with a professional like me.

EMERGENCY QUESTIONS

1. Would you prefer to have a hand made out of ham or an armpit that dispensed sun cream?
NB The hand would grow back each time you ate it and would function perfectly as a hand, though it would leave a greasy residue on everything it touched. The sun cream would be of a factor of your choosing and be enough for your own personal use but not enough to bottle and sell.

2. If you had to have sex with an animal – if you _had_ to – what animal would you have sex with and why?
Rich: I'd choose the okapi. From behind it looks like a lady wearing zebra-print trousers and it's also got a surprisingly long tongue. If I had to, I mean. If I had to.

3. Have you ever seen a ghost?

Interesting fact for after the question has been answered: ghosts do not exist. Anyone who says they have seen one is thus mentally imbalanced.

4. Have you ever seen a Bigfoot?

NB If someone starts telling you about the time they saw a sasquatch or a yeti, immediately stop them talking. The question is: Have you ever seen a Bigfoot?

5. If an Emergency Question is asked in a forest, but the person who asks it is immediately crushed to death by a falling tree, do you still have to answer? What if you didn't quite hear it over the sound of the falling tree?

Rich: Please use this book responsibly if you are in a forest or wooded area of any kind. Check that it is safe to ask a question.

6. Isn't silver actually better than gold?

Rich: Miles better. And bronze is the best, which is why my bronze Sony Award is so special to me. Three is also higher than one, too!

7. **What is your favourite cheese?**
Rich: Sorry to my home town of Cheddar, but no question, it's halloumi. Any other answer is incorrect.

8. **Has your sibling ever seen a ghost?**

9. **Who is your favourite historical character?**
Rich: The pretender to the English throne: Perkin Warbeck.

10. **What do you think happens when we die?**
Rich: I believe whatever you believe will happen when you die, that's what happens – which is an organisational nightmare for God. He has to knock up new heavens every five minutes based on the whim of lunatics.

11

11. If you could choose one thing for your armpit to dispense, what would that thing be?

12. Would you rather be a cow or a badger?

NB This question reveals a surprising amount about whether a person prefers conformity or freedom. Or being milked or gassed by farmers.

13. What age were you breastfed until?

Rich: Most people won't remember, but, boy, have you hit pay dirt if you find someone who does.

14. If you had to marry a Muppet – if you *had* to – which Muppet would you marry?

Rich: Funella from *The Furchester Hotel*. My wife says this is okay as long as I can persuade the puppeteer and voice-over artiste to be in on the arrangement to make the whole experience authentic. As if I wasn't going to do that anyway. I don't want to have sex with a limp Muppet – I want it moving around and talking. That's the whole point!

15. Have you ever had a near death experience?

16. Would you rather have a tit that dispenses talcum powder or a finger that can travel through 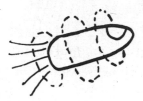 **time? What would you do with such a power?**
NB You would produce limitless talcum powder so could sell it for profit. Only your finger travels through time. You'd be able to look through the hole to see what was going on, but only your finger could interact.

17. What's the worst experience you've ever had in a hotel?
Rich: In a hotel in Cambridge I found someone else's bogey on my shower curtain.

18. Which celebrity would you like to stroke your hair as you die?
Rich: I think I chose Bouncer from *Neighbours*. Or Goldie from *Blue Peter*. I don't know why.

19. Do you have a favourite towel? What is your best story about it?

Rich: I do. It's Old Bluey. Portly comedian Andre Vincent once borrowed it without asking when he stayed in our flat in Edinburgh and I've never been able to enjoy using it again.

20. What is your most mundane encounter with a celebrity?

Rich: One of the blokes who used to be in *Hollyoaks* and who I think is now in *Casualty*, and who might be married to Topsy and Tim's mum in real life, once said 'Hello' to me thinking he knew me, but then realised he'd just seen me on TV.

21. How sensitive are your nipples?

NB Take a chance – if you're on a date, make that the first question you ask. Don't even say 'Hello'.

22. **Would you rather date a man who is a six foot tall penis or a man who instead of having a penis has a tiny man there?**

NB The six-foot penis man would have a face on his helmet, but otherwise is just a huge penis (without balls). He would be wearing a suit jacket with false arms on it to give himself a more human appearance. The tiny man would be living with his feet implanted in his host man but would be a separate individual with his own personality. He in turn would have a tiny man instead of a penis and so on to infinity.

23. **Have you ever come up with an idea for conceptual or performance art that you think is better than any of the guff that gets nominated for the Turner Prize?**

Rich: Walk a Mile in my Shoes – every pair of shoes a person ever owned in their life, from cradle to grave, stuck to the floor along a promenade a mile long. Also, *Me1 versus Me2 Snooker* – an ongoing podcast in which I play myself at snooker badly and commentate on it badly (released on audio only).

24. Are you ever mistaken for a celebrity? Which one?

Rich: Hideous motorcycle freak Charley Boorman. Ironically, he genuinely advertises Herring Shoes, and I think he only got the gig because they thought he was me.

25. Do you have any good ideas for terrorist atrocities?

Rich: Explosives in Berocca form that you can just add to water on the aircraft. Or boob bombs. I have loads of these. I am prepared to sell to the highest bidder. Obviously I hope that the anti-terrorist forces will be the ones to pay for this information, to avoid loss of life. And if they don't, then I hope they can sleep at night.

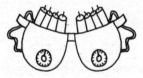

26. What's the best advice you've ever received and ignored?

27. Have you ever had the opportunity to assassinate a public figure?

Rich: Yes, Michael Gove. At least twice. My apologies for failing both times. Also, I found myself in a dark corridor at 1 a.m. once, right behind an unprotected Nigel Farage.

28. Does sex with a robot count as cheating on your partner?

Rich: No.

Rich's wife: Yes.

29. Why can't everyone be babies?

30. Kettle crisps* are not as nice as they once were. Have I changed, or have they? DON'T LET THEM ANSWER THAT! IT'S RHETORICAL. If you could travel back in time to compare any food of today with an equivalent of the past: What time would you choose? Which food?

31. If you had to go on a week's holiday with a *Spitting Image* puppet – if you *had* to – which one would you choose?

NB Bear in mind that the puppet would choose the holiday destination and both the puppeteer and voice-over artist would also come with you, but you would not be able to communicate with them directly, only as the puppet.

32. Is sex with a ghost cheating?

---

* I refuse to call them Kettle Chips as I am not American and am also convinced that they were originally called Kettle Crisps in the UK. Kettle deny it, but various investigations by fans of the podcast have discovered records showing the company was once called that. What are they trying to hide?

33. Should penis transplants ever be allowed? What are the possible terrifying consequences of such a procedure in your opinion?

Rich: I just fear that a rich man would harvest my beautiful penis for his own use before I have finished with it.

34. Would you rather date a woman who is a six-foot vulva, or a woman who instead of having genitalia has another woman living in a burrow between her legs?

35. What's your worst experience with the delivery company Yodel? Is there a worse delivery company in existence?

36. What's the best museum you've ever been to?
Rich: Keswick's Pencil Museum.

37. What age would you like to be when you get to heaven, presuming there is a heaven and you get to choose what age you'll be when you're up there?

NB I am not asking what age you will be when you die, just what age you'd like to revert to when you are walking/flying around in heaven.

38. If you could get a law named after you, what would it be?

Rich: Herring's Law is that whatever locker you choose at the gym, when you come back to it, the person at the next-door locker will be there getting their stuff in or out and be in your way.

39. If you could have a part of the human body named after you, what would it be?

Rich: I would like the external meatus (what kids at my school used to offensively call 'The Jap's Eye') renamed as 'The Herring's Eye'.

40. What do you consider your median achievement?

41. Do you ever worry that you have already lived your life and are now in a care home with Alzheimer's Disease and what you perceive as reality is just a distorted memory of the first time this happened?

42. Have you ever tried sushi?

43. Have you ever tried sashimi?

44. Have you ever flown a kite?

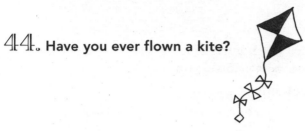

45. Have you ever demolished a wall or a building?

46. What's the worst incorrect rumour you have heard about yourself?

Rich: That I invite women back to my hotel room and make them dance whilst I sit in a high-backed armchair and masturbate. I have never done this and anyone who says I have is lying.

47. Why do we have frozen peas? Why is that vegetable predominantly used in frozen form? I know there are other frozen veg, but only the pea is principally used as a frozen rather than fresh or tinned commodity. Why?

48. Have you ever been in the vicinity of a Bigfoot, but not seen it, and sensed it watching you?

49. Where do you stand on transubstantiation?

50. If you were given the powers of a King Midas, what would you turn everything you touched into?

Rich: I would make everything I touch turn into the thing that it already is, but now holding or covered in diamonds which I would then be given. Of course, once I had the diamonds they would turn into more diamonds with diamonds on them, but I wouldn't be too bothered by that.

51. If you had the powers of a Gary Sparrow and could travel from the nineties to the forties, what would you do?

52. Would you rather have a tongue that could taste impending danger or get a free iPhone?

53. **Do you know the way to San Jose?**
Rich: Not from here, no.

54. **I once burped during the minute's silence at the Ascension Day Service. What was the most audacious thing you did whilst at school/during a minute's silence?**

55. **Would you rather do a *Freaky Friday* vice versa with Brian Blessed or CJ from *Eggheads*?**
NB You would be back to yourself after the day was over and would not be culpable for any crimes you had pretended to commit or lies about going to Mars.

56. **Which conspiracy theory do you think might actually be true? Come on, one of them must be! And the others were just made up to make that one look just as crazy.**
Rich: I think Paul McCartney was replaced by a lookalike with slightly different ears in the sixties.

57. How do you sleep at night?

58. What do you consider to be the most mediocre chocolate bar?

Rich: Definitely a Twix. It is nobody's favourite or least favourite snack.

59. What happened to Lazarus the second time he died?

60. If a serial killer kills another serial killer, does that work like conkers?

61. What is your favourite keyboard shortcut?

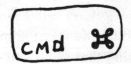

62. Would you rather have no ears or no dignity?

63. If you had to, would you rather give up chocolate or cheese – if you *had* to?

64. If you had the power to bring down planes with your mind, would you be able to resist doing so just once? Just to check you really could? Or would you do it loads anyway, laughing at the destruction you had wrought?

65. What modern-day item do you think will seem ridiculously archaic in ten years' time?

66. What is the most embarrassing thing you've ever tried to squeeze down the drain in a shower?
Rich: Some poo. It was my own, so that's not so bad. But, in a way, that's also worse.

67. If you were in a *Groundhog Day* situation, what would be the worst crime that you would commit, knowing that when you woke up it would almost certainly not have happened?

68. If you had to bathe in excrement – if you *had* to – what animal or particular human's excrement would you choose to bathe in?

69. If you were God, what flavour would you have made ejaculate?

Because it's like God didn't even consider that people were going to eat it.

70. Do you ever worry that you're a character in a computer game operated by some bored teenage deity or alien who is deliberately just making loads of shit happen to see what you'll do, like you're nothing more than an ant under a microscope, and soon he'll get bored and have you killed in a ridiculous way? Because I do.

71. If you had to be killed in a natural disaster – if you *had* to – which natural disaster would you choose?

Rich: If I *had* to, I would be killed in a Vesuvius-like volcanic explosion and would try to get into a funny pose so that I'd make future archaeologists laugh when they made a plaster-cast statue from the space I left in the ash.

72. Who is the most impressive celebrity who ever came to your school?
Rich: Rick Buckler, the drummer from The Jam, was the brother of our art teacher and he once played in our school hall with his arguably less successful band Time UK.

73. Did any future celebrities go to your school?
Rich: Jack Bessant, the bassist from Reef.

74. Did any siblings of celebrities teach at your school?
Rich: Yes, Mr Buckler, the art teacher, was the brother of Rick Buckler from The Jam. I said that two questions ago. Why aren't you paying attention?

75. What is your preferred epithet for male genitalia?
Rich: The Honourable Member for Fuckinghamshire.

76. What is your preferred epithet for female genitalia?

Rich: Clackerlackadackdack.

77. Could you ever have sex with someone that calls breasts 'boobies'? What if they did it while you were having sex? Would you stop having sex with them?

Rich: I would definitely stop. I don't mind if someone calls them boobs, though. It's weird.

78. If I could guarantee that you would be unkillable, indestructible and uninjurable for the next ten years, but that you would die once the decade was up, would you go for it?

79. When you have fears that you may cease to be before your pen has gleaned your teeming brain, what do you do?

Rich: Write stuff down more quickly. Think how many sonnets selfish John Keats denied us by his tardy penmanship.

80. Have you ever stolen a golf buggy?

81. What's your favourite drink? If you found out that it was actually made out of wasp urine and always had been, would it still be your favourite, and would you carry on drinking it?

82. Would you rather be immune from ever getting chlamydia or have free KitKats for life? (You would get 365 four-finger KitKats per year, or 366 on a Leap Year, but would still be able to get chlamydia).

83. If you could go into the transportation chamber from *The Fly* with a living creature of your choice, which creature would you choose?
Rich: An okapi, as long as I got to be the human top half and the okapi bottom half, like a sexy okapi centaur.

84. If you could have a sex robot resembling any human living or dead, who would that be?

NB Even if the person is dead the sex robot will be 'alive'.

Rich: I would have a sex robot of my wife, so that I could still have sex with her even when she is away … Has my wife stopped reading this now? Good. It would be Gemma Chan.

85. If you had a silo, what would you store in it?

Rich: Baked beans … so I could always eat baked beans.

86. If you got the chance, would you cryogenically freeze yourself at the point of death in the hope of being cured in the future? How do you think you'd fit in if it worked out for you? Would you be worried that future humans would think you were a primitive idiot?

87. What's the most pretentious book you've ever bought, but never read?

Rich: I have some prominently displayed James Joyce on my bookshelf and have never read a word.

88. If everyone else in the world departed in a space ship and left you behind so that everything belonged to you, where would you live? What paintings would you have on your wall? Would you be lonely? Where would be the most ostentatious place you would masturbate?

89. Are you the postman or the letterbox?

90. Is the glass half full or half empty? And what does it say about you if you're too afraid to ask someone straight whether they're an optimist or a pessimist, instead using a confusing glass metaphor? You haven't even said what's in the glass. What if it's a glass of poison? You've learned nothing about us, but we have learned a lot about you.

91. If you were Adam Sandler, how would you even begin to spend the millions of dollars you made for appearing in *The Cobbler*?

Rich: I would build a silo and fill it with baked beans so that I never had to buy food again.

92. Do you make a mental file of answers that would work well if you ever appeared on *Pointless*?

Rich: Of course, doesn't everyone? If you get Kevin Spacey films then say *Heartburn*. He probably won't come up now though.

93. When you're watching films, how much time do you end up Googling the actors to find out if they are still alive and then annoy your wife by talking about it and saying 'Dead' if the actor is dead?

Rich: Yes, I do exactly that. How did you know? It's like this book has been written specifically for me.

94. Have you ever been in a canoe?

95. Have you ever had a dream that accurately predicted the future?

101 EMERGENCY QUESTIONS FOR DATES

In 2004 I did a stand-up show where I took on a series of Herculean feats. One was to go on fifty dates with fifty different people to fifty different places in fifty consecutive days. It was a crazy, drunken, emotionally confusing and hedonistic month and a half. Most of the dates were with people who I didn't know and who were friends of friends who just happened to be single. There was no attempt to matchmake or any expectation of romance. The only criterion was that the person was prepared to spend a night out with a comedian who was dating forty-nine other people in the same two-month period. Bizarrely, this lack of expectation and frivolity made for the perfect dating situation, and I met several people with whom I might have liked to be in a relationship if only I hadn't had to date another stranger the next night, and the next, and the next . . . It was a confusing time.

However, I learned some stuff about what makes a good and a bad date, and the mistakes that people seem to make. The worst error, made particularly by men, is to treat a date as a chance to monologue about how great you are, which is a shame, because the real purpose of the date is to show how interested you are in the other person (or, if you are cynical and an idiot, to appear like you're interested). Fellas, if you have the consideration to just ask some questions then you will immediately seem like an extraordinarily good date.

Also, wash before the date. If you don't have time to have a full wash, then wash the smellier areas and work outwards from there. If you ask questions *and* wash, then you put yourself in the top ten per cent of dates. The rest is up to you.

People tend to ask the same questions on dates and some of them have their place, as you probably want to know a bit about the other person's work or their family, but they probably won't lead to very interesting conversations. Lots of the questions in this book can be used in a dating context, but here are 101 that I have specifically written with a first date in mind. Some of them are a bit flirty or silly, but others may get you on to more philosophical areas (though hopefully without getting into subjects like politics or religion, which you might want to avoid for now). A couple of them are deliberately outrageous and you should use those with caution (though if the date is going well they might add the extra fizz you require). If they go down badly, you can always blame me and bond with your date about what an idiot I am. I am very good at this wingman role in real life. I can make you look amazing in comparison to me.

Oh, and don't just ask the questions: listen to the answers (or, if you're an idiot, pretend to) and ask subsidiary questions. You won't believe how effective being an engaged and interested human being is in making you attractive.

96. What is the worst date you've ever been on?
Rich: I took someone to Garfunkel's in Leicester Square, which turned out to be the most embarrassing dining experience ever, and then we went to see *Starsky and Hutch* at the cinema which turned out to be the worst film ever. But sometimes a shared terrible experience is as bonding as a good one, especially after such a disappointment.

97. If you had to go out with a vampire, a werewolf, a leprechaun or a shrek, which supernatural creature would you go out with and where would you go?
Rich: I would choose a shrek (which I understand is a specific species of ogre. This is not the same as the character Shrek from the film franchise *Shrek*, who is a shrek who happens also to be called Shrek).
NB Anyone attracted to vampires and werewolves is strange, as they want to kill you. I know you think you can change them, but you can't. You might as well

marry a serial killer, you saddo. A leprechaun is rich and won't murder you, but hates humanity and will play tricks on you throughout the date, and will never let you dip in his pot. A shrek is a horrible, flatulent and stinking being, but there is only about a fifty per cent chance of being murdered and he'll probably let you bum him on a first date.

98. What's the most impulsive thing you've ever done?

99. What's the worst thing that's ever happened to you when you've been kissing?
Rich: **The other person was sick. We cleaned up and carried on.**

100. If you had to go on a date with a character from *The Simpsons*, which character would you choose and why?
Rich: **I'd quite like a threesome with Itchy and Scratchy – those guys are into anything – though I might insist on a safe word. And Poochy is not allowed to watch.**

101. What was your most devastating unrequited teenage crush?

Rich: Almost all of them, but I loved Maria Barnes, and Adam Baker told me that she wanted me to ask her out. He was lying. I asked her out and she (very nicely) refused and then had a go at Adam Baker about it . . . not that I remember every detail of it and every scintilla of pain.

102. Who was the first person you remember fancying?

Rich: As a young child I remember being intrigued by Barry Manilow, Nana Mouskouri, the blonde one from Abba and the blonde one from The Sweet. What can I say? I liked musicians.

103. What is your greatest achievement (that most people wouldn't think was that great)?

NB Feel free to just ask the first bit as it's nice to let people show off on a date, but the bit in brackets might give you a better idea of what they are like.

Rich: I played the word 'equators' across two triple word scores in Scrabble. SEE?

104. Do you think someone on a date asking you questions from a book is brilliant or a bit tragic?
Rich: It's clearly brilliant. If they say 'tragic', make a mental note not to have sex with them (unless they are very sexy). If they say 'brilliant', make a mental note to have sex with them. Oh, you have already.

105. Which children's story, song or TV show do you think is most fundamentally flawed?
Rich: I am at a loss to understand how Postman Pat remains employed when he screws up every delivery, let alone why he has been given so many vehicles to make deliveries. Also, I am very troubled by the whole *Cinderella* story – why did the Fairy Godmother only allow Cinderella to have the magic stuff until midnight? Either help out or don't.

106. Where is your most surprising erogenous zone?
NB Maybe don't start with this question.

107. What's the most unusual restaurant you've ever been to?
Rich: I went on a date to a Polish-Mexican restaurant. Sadly, it was either Polish *or* Mexican dishes, rather than an attempt to combine the two.

108. What thing that seemingly everyone else likes do you think is a bit rubbish?
Rich: Superhero movies. They're okay for kids, but why are so many adults watching them? And actually, graphic novels as well. Same deal.

109. What thing that you *should* regret do you not regret?
Rich: I regret never having sung '*Je Ne Regrette Rien*' at karaoke.

110. Shall we have/adopt children together?
NB This one will sort out the serious from the non-serious and probably ensure you never have sex again.

111. Which non-potato crisp is the best?
Rich: It's obviously pickled onion Monster Munch, but if you eat those before a date then you are worse than Hitler.

112. Where is the most unusual place that you have ever made out?

Rich: Sadly I am generally quite unadventurous in this regard. Oh . . . I once made out with an actress in the dressing room of a comedy show I was in. We were both dressed as the characters we played. I wasn't sure if I was meant to be me or still meant to be acting. I think she wanted me to be the character, but the joke's on her, because I was actually still being me!

113. Do you believe in anything supernatural?

114. Are men and women really that different or are we all just conforming to the expectations of society?

115. What is your favourite swear-word?

Rich: Spunkbucket.

116. What is the worst thing that has happened to you on holiday?
Rich: I was knocked over by a wave in Barbados and hit my head, and for some reason one of my testicles swelled up to four times its normal (very impressive) size. On the flight home it worked as quite an efficient altimeter – the higher we went, the more it hurt.

117. Which species of animal has the most impressive mating ritual?

118. Do you think that opposites attract? And even if they do, do you think that makes for a good relationship? What is the most opposite couple you can imagine?
Rich: Hitler and Mother Teresa. I think it might have worked. Trump and Princess Di – he says that nearly happened. Maybe sometimes people we think of as opposite are more similar than they appear.

119. What do you like best about me so far?
NB Try to deliver this in a cool Han Solo way, rather than a needy 'please love me' way. Actually, don't risk it. You don't know how you come across.

120. When people find out what you do for a living, what is the most annoying thing that they say? *Rich:* 'Tell us a joke.' Mainly because I don't know any, and it reveals to everyone that I am delusional to think that that is my job.

121. What is your biggest weakness?
Rich: Addiction to Twirls . . . and the sound that polystyrene makes when it is rubbed against polystyrene. If anyone says that their biggest weakness is that they have no weaknesses, then immediately get up, walk out and never look back.

122. What's your favourite shop?

123. What would be the worst place that you can imagine going to on a first date?
Rich: Texas Fried Chicken on the Goldhawk Road in Shepherd's Bush . . . even if you had pre-booked the one table that they have. Or maybe that restaurant in Leicester Square.

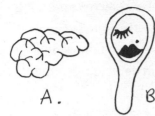

A.   B.

124. What is more important to you: brains or beauty?
Rich: The truth is that anyone without a brain is not going to be able to function on any level. Anyone choosing beauty first probably doesn't care that they will be hanging around with a blow-up doll or scarecrow, though.

125. If you could have a sexual superpower, what would it be?

126. Do you prefer things to be planned or spontaneous?
Rich: Let me have a think about that and I will get back to you.

127. What's the most stupid thing you've done for love?

128. What's the most unusual thing that you've ever collected?

129. Who is your most eccentric relative and what is the most eccentric thing they have done?

130. What is your most interesting quirk?

131. Who was your favourite Gladiator?

132. Do big romantic gestures make you happy or embarrassed?

133. If you kiss enough frogs, will you end up with a prince or just some kind of amphibian mouth illness or poisoned lips?

134. What's the most disgusting thing that you've ever had in your mouth?

135. Do you have lucky knickers? Are you wearing them now?

136. Are you already in a relationship with someone else?
Rich: This might not matter to you, but it's important to be open and honest on a date. And this might save trouble down the line.

137. How do you imagine people managed to fix up dates before Tinder?

138. If you had to live in the burrow or nest of an animal for a week, which animal's home would you live in?

139a. Would you like to give me oral sex? WARNING: Only ask this first if you want this to be an incredibly short date, one way or the other. Alternatively, try:

139b. Would you like me to give you oral sex? Which will at least make you look like a giving person . . . and also make this a short date, one way or the other.

140. I like your hair ... but what was your most disastrous haircut?

WARNING: Don't say the first bit to a bald person. Or probably the second bit.

Rich: When I was five, after watching a hairdressing segment on *The Generation Game*, I attempted to cut my own hair. It worked out slightly worse than you are imagining.

141. Isn't it best just to get the sex out of the way as soon as possible in a relationship to discover if there is anything more than physical attraction going on?

Rich: It's worth a try.

142. What is your philosophy?

Rich: My enemy's enemy is my friend. Unfortunately, as it turns out, my enemy is his own worst enemy.

143. If I said you had a beautiful body would you tell me I should ask for a refund from the author of this book?

Rich: No refunds.

144. Have you ever been on a motorboat?

145. Have you ever used or had used upon you the chat-up line: 'Did you hurt yourself ... when you fell from heaven?' Because isn't it actually an insult? Doesn't it heavily imply that the questioner thinks that you were ejected from heaven for some misdemeanour like Satan? If you were an angel you would have floated down using your wings and been fine. Also, aren't most angels terrifying-looking babies? Aren't manufactured chat-up lines all just awful?
Rich: Hopefully they won't spot that this is a manufactured chat-up line.

146. You are dressed so well tonight, but what was the worst fashion decision you ever made?
Rich: I experimented with a centre parting.

147. What convention of our society do you wish no longer existed?
Rich: I find it weird that we're so concerned about bodily hair and eradicating it. I am proud to be a mammal. Ditto about my ability to lactate.

148. What mistake do you keep making again and again?

149. Are you handy?
NB This question is deliberately ambiguous and the way it is taken can tell you a lot about a person.

150. What do you make of the strangers around us? What do you imagine their lives and relationships are like?
NB Make sure you whisper to each other so that the strangers don't hear.

151. What have you recently done for the first time?

152. What if the stars had been made just for us, to illuminate our walk home tonight?

153. Have you ever been on a date with someone who is secretly royalty or a millionaire but who is pretending not to be so that they can be sure your romantic interest is sincere?
NB When they say no, pull a face that suggests that maybe there's something they don't know about you.

154. If I had food on my face or stuck in my teeth, would you tell me about it?

155. If you could be any sitcom character, which sitcom character would you be?

156. What is the sexiest language?
NB Whatever language they say, speak fluently to them in that language. You will need to learn all the languages before the date for this to work. If you are on Tinder, just use Google translate.

157. Would you rather have a fancy kitchen or a big garden?

158. Do you believe in fate? Would you accept that if fate exists then free will is non-existent and we consequently have no choice over any of our actions? So, shall we have sex anyway?

159. What's the biggest creature that you've had to get out of your house?
Rich: There was a huge crow flying around in an upstairs bedroom the other day. It was the most terrifying thing that has ever happened to me.
I screamed like a baby but managed to open a window in the end and it escaped.

160. What word that you've seen written down do you not know how to pronounce?
Rich: Opprobrium.

161. A friend of mine's parents told her that if an ice cream van's music was playing it meant they had run out of ice cream. What light-hearted lie did your parents tell you and how long did it take for you to realise that it wasn't true?

162. What's the best thing that you've ever done in the rain?

163. Is there a catchphrase from an old TV show or advert that hardly anyone else remembers but that you still use on a regular basis?
Rich: I constantly say, 'Your girlfriend is going to love your oniony breath,' which comes from a nineties chewing gum advert.

164. Who is the most famous person you have been in a swimming pool with?
Rich: Toby Anstis. I don't know him. He was just using the same pool as me.

165. Would you be prepared to have elephants' ears replacing your own ears if the elephant ears gave you the power to hear anything within a fifty-metre radius (and could also be used to cool yourself down and make yourself appear more threatening in dangerous situations)?
Rich: No, I think that these limited uses would not overcome the difficulty of finding a hat that fitted and keeping my spectacles on.

166. Do you feel immortality would be a desirable thing? Wouldn't a never-ending life eventually become an unbearable hell?

167. Which celebrity do you consider to have the stupidest name?
Rich: Engelbert Humperdinck (though not the pop singer, I am referring to the German composer from whom he stole his name).

168. If you had to have a bath with a member of East 17, but only one member, which one of the quartet would you bathe with?
Rich: The one who stood at the back and did that thing with his hands and had a funny moustache.

169. If you could resurrect a woolly mammoth, what would you knit with its wool?

170. What things do you do online that you would never do in real life?

171. Do you prefer coffee or aeroplanes? If you had to choose to eradicate one of the two from all human history, which would go? Coffee or aeroplanes?

172. Which subject were you worst at at school?
Rich: Art. I hated it so much that I got my middle-school art folder and burned everything I had created over the previous four years. It was a stupid thing to do and says a lot about me, and I regret it terribly.

173. What thing do you most regret destroying with fire?
Rich: My middle-school art folder.

174. What are we doing after this?

175. Is there something you once abhorred that you now adore?
Rich: As a child I hated the smell of coffee so much that I had to run past the shop in Weston-super-Mare High Street that sold ground coffee. Now I love coffee so much I would destroy all aeroplanes now and throughout history to ensure its survival.

176. Do you have a favourite joke?

Rich: Yes, it's the one with the punchline: 'Lemon entry, my dear Watson'.

177. Which is the best of the cartoon cats?

Rich: Tough one. Liono is the toughest, but Top Cat is the coolest. Don't make me choose.

178. What's your most impressive party trick?

Rich: I can recite the first page of the New Testament. If you can do this too, please don't do it on a date or you are guaranteed to die a virgin.

179. What was the strangest thing you've done on a date that has actually impressed the person you're with?

Rich: In Pizza Express I ordered the Veneziana pizza and then told the waiter that I did not want the discretionary 25p to go to the Venice in Peril charity because I hated Venice and wanted it to sink. This created just the right amount of confusion amongst the staff and laughter from my date to create an interesting and spontaneous moment, and I dated that woman for the next eighteen months. Then I tried it again on another date and it worked then too. Maybe just do this on all your dates.

180. Do you secretly hate Venice and wish they would just let it sink into the sea where it belongs?

Rich: No, I like it, really. I just pretended I didn't to show off, but it's still a fun question to ask out of the blue. If that question offends your date, you can say, 'Hey, it's not my question, and I agree with you, whoever made that up is a monster.' If they like the question then pretend you made it up. That's the beauty of Emergency Questions. You're off the hook.

181. Do you still have any friends from school or college?

182. Have you ever bled a radiator?
Rich: Yes, and at least once the screw has come out and spewed dirty radiator water all over my carpets and curtains.

183. What is the most impressive meal that you can cook from scratch?
Rich: My skills are limited, but I do a mean vegetable chilli.

184. Which person who you've never met has had the greatest influence on your life?
Rich: I stood behind him at a petrol station but didn't introduce myself, and I wish I had, so I think I can still say Rik Mayall.

185. Have you ever been in the proximity of one of your heroes and been too shy to say anything to them?
Rich: I stood behind Rik Mayall at a petrol station. Why didn't I just say, 'Hello. You are ace!'?

186. What's the most unusual thing that you've ever rented?

187. What musical instrument that you don't know how to play do you think you could pick up right now and have a pretty good crack at?
Rich: The trombone looks like a doddle.

188. What's the naughtiest thing you've ever done?
Rich: I once ran through a field of wheat . . . after running over a child whilst drunk. My publisher has asked me to point out that this is not true and merely a humorous parody of a remark made by the UK prime minister (as we went to press) Theresa May.

189. What's your most common recurring dream?
Rich: I am constantly re-taking my A-Levels.
Last night, as a change of pace, I was getting my
O-Level results (for O-Levels that I was taking again for
some reason, even though I'd done much better
the first time).

190. Is your happiest memory of a time when you
were alone or with other people?

191. Are humans ultimately selfish beings?

192. What's the most embarrassing photo of you
that your family have on display?

193. What was the last picture that you took on
your phone? Are you happy to show it to me?
Rich: Mine is of my daughter pretending to drink from a
tiny cocktail glass that is supposed to go in the bottom
of a fish tank.

194. What is the most slapstick thing that has ever happened to you?

Rich: My cat had knocked a box of drawing pins on to the floor and I stood on one, yelped, moved my foot and stood on another one. Then I knelt down to remove the pins and landed on yet another.

195. Which supposedly attractive film star do you think is a bit ugly?
Rich: George Clooney. He has a tortoise's mouth. The most testudinate lips I've seen this side of the Galapagos Islands.

196. This isn't exactly a job interview, but it's a bit like it in a way, so do you have any questions you'd like to ask me?

197. Do you secretly wonder if you are the new Jesus? Maybe you are.

198. You know when you wake up in the middle of the night with a feeling of inexplicable existential dread – you're not sure why you're so panicked but it feels like life is meaningless and terrible and pointless: what if that's the only time you have any kind of mental clarity?

199. What is your favourite pinball table?

Rich: If the answer is anything but *The Addams Family* Pinball then you are WRONG. If your answer is 'What's a pinball table?' then all your future answers are void.

200. Did you ever go camping with your family? What are your abiding memories of that awful experience?

Rich: I fancied a Dutch girl called Carla and snogged with her after I had accidentally fallen into a lake in the dark. It was the best experience of my life. I touched her boobies ... Oh no, I've become one of the people who says boobies.

201. Which is best: Cheddar Caves or Wookey Hole?

Rich: Cheddar Caves is the correct answer, even though Wookey Hole is objectively better.

202. If you had to do a human centipede with two other people – if you *had to* – and you were in the middle, which two people would you choose and at which end would each go?

Rich: I would like my mouth attached to Gemma Chan's anus and my anus attached to Michael Gove's mouth. That way no one has to put their lips on Michael Gove's anus – something that has, as yet, never happened and never should. Also, Gemma Chan's poop would almost certainly be delicious, but its deliciousness would be sullied by the time it has gone through me.

203. Do you remember the first time that a childhood enthusiasm was crushed and broken?

Rich: I had been at my first disco at Fairlands Middle School and had danced the night away. I was sweating from the exuberance of my exertions and went outside. I remember the cold air biting into me, but I didn't care. I was happy. Then Steve Cheeke said, 'You were terrible at dancing.' I have never enjoyed dancing since.

204. What is your favourite archaic word or phrase?

Rich: In the Middle Ages they used to call a skirt 'a fuck-sail'.

205. Who do you consider the most appalling member of Margaret Thatcher's Cabinet (excluding Margaret Thatcher obviously)?

Rich: Cecil Parkinson – the way he conducted his personal life was appalling. However, I met him about two weeks before he died, and he was avuncular and charming.

206. How many different human beings' poo have you had to deal with?

Rich: I think actually only mine and my kids' . . . Oh no, wait, also whoever it was who did a shit by my front gate last year. Probably some others, too, now I think about it. Oh yeah, I mean if you include *THAT*, yeah.

207. Which is your favourite
bun that is named after a place?
Rich: The Chelsea bun is
pretty good.

208. If you had to marry a piece of furniture –
if you *had* to – which piece of furniture would
you marry?
Rich: I would marry the Coronation Chair that is in
Westminster Abbey, but only if they reinstate the
Stone of Scone into the base.

209. Who is the most evil person you
have ever met?
Rich: I didn't meet him, but I once briefly stayed in
a hotel room that had just been vacated by President
Assad of Syria.

210. What does 'mansplaining' mean?
NB Ask a man this question and then when he
starts explaining shout 'Stop mansplaining!'
and tut loudly.

211. When you are asked to imagine a time or place when you are calm and happy, what time and/or place do you imagine?

Rich: I go back to a holiday I had in Thailand where I was staying in a beach hut and one night at midnight noticed that a small sand-bank had appeared a few metres out to sea. My drunk girlfriend of the time went to bed, but I took a plastic chair and sat on this little island (which I called 'Chard Island' after a pretentious shortening of my own first name) and watched the moon crossing the sky.

DAVID MITCHELL

David Mitchell is perhaps the ideal guest for my podcast as he treats me as though I am an intelligent six-year-old child, and takes the time to answer my questions both extremely thoroughly and as if they are in any way reasonable. He also out-Emergency-Questioned my Emergency Questions by adding subsidiary questions – such as asking whether paper would become translucent if he picked it up with his ham hand – which is absolutely what everyone should be doing with this book. Here are eight questions based on two interviews with David:

212. David once played table tennis with Aerosmith. What's the most unlikely activity that you have participated in with a celebrity or celebrities?

213. On *Dirty Britcom Confessions* (a website in which people anonymously post their sexual fantasies about UK-based comedians) someone claimed they wanted to dip David Mitchell in mayonnaise from head to foot and then have Rich Herring lick it all off. Which pair of incongruous celebrities would you like to see licking sauce or condiments off each other? Who would be the licker and who the lickee? And what would the lickee be coated in?

214. Rich and David discussed talking dirty in bed. Do you swear during sex?
David: No, you swear a lot when you do DIY. It's already so rude having sex. You're really being very rude, so there's no need to gild that particular lily of filth.
Rich: If anything, just a quiet apology for what you're doing.

215. If you had to list *Peep Show* episodes from least favourite to most favourite, which would be the mean (i.e. average) episode?
David: So many average ones to choose from. I'm immediately thinking of the sectioning episode from Series 3, which I always thought was pretty good, but not my favourite.

216. Rich and David were both new fathers at the time of their second interview and discussed how babies are incapable of doing anything wrong as they have no understanding of morality. Is there a greater philosophical tragedy than the loss of this innocence?

217. David used to work in the cloakroom for Chris Evans' TV show *TFI Friday*, which involved looking after the bags and coats of the audience who never had as good a time as they thought they would. What job have you had that sounded glamorous but was unbearably tedious?

218. Rich told David about a family of shreks he had seen on Westminster Bridge trying to cajole tourists into having their photo taken with them. What is the most unsettling or aggressive street performer you have ever seen?

219. The *Daily Mail* online has run two stories about David and his wife taking their child on a walk in a pram. What is the most mundane event you have read in a newspaper article?

220. **If you could have a dream dinner party with any person living or dead, who would you employ to do the washing up?**

NB They would not be allowed to join the dinner party, but would get tantalising snippets of the conversation that always cut off before the interesting bit/punchline.

221. **If you dropped your mobile phone down the Portaloo on Day 3 of Glastonbury Festival, would you retrieve it?**

222. **What has been the worst occasion in which you have been totally naked?**

Rich: During my play *Excavating Rita* I would be naked every night. It was a humiliating episode for the character I played, and the audience usually got it and it was a funny moment, but one time they didn't really react so it felt like *I* was naked rather than the character and I was embarrassed. The character then gets punched out and usually I got a cloth thrown over me, but when the actor threw the cloth it missed, and so I was lying on the floor with my pathetic genitals on display and unable to do anything to cover myself. I suppose it was my own fault for writing it.

223. Who are your three
favourite ghosts, real or (let's
face it) fictional?
Rich: Timothy Claypole, Anne
Boleyn and the New Shmoo
(who I assume is a ghost).

224. Shag, marry or kill? Oxygen, ennui,
mitochondria?

225. Would you rather be killed by being shot out
of a cannon, dropped into a well, or impaled on a
giant spike that you have to sit on top of and then
very slowly descend on to via your anus?

226. Are you a racist?
NB They'll probably say no, but you might
catch one out.

227. Have you ever appeared on a TV quiz show?
If so, please tell me in excruciating detail about how
you got on, especially if you lost . . .
Rich: I have, but I don't like to talk about it.

228. Do you think they will ever make a *Hunger Games*-style film based around the ITV daytime quiz show *Tipping Point?*

229. What is the strangest thing you have found in your cleavage, belly button or anal cleft?

230. Have you planned out what you would do in the event of a zombie apocalypse?
Rich: I would hide and wait for the zombies to grind to a halt and rot away. I have a baked bean silo in my house so would not need to leave it for sustenance.

231. Which seemingly respectable celebrity do you suspect is a coked-up sex pest?
Rich: Redacted O' redacted!

232. What is your favourite Papal name?
Rich: Boniface ... No, Urban ... It's so hard to choose.

233. Would you like to be a professional cricketer?

234. Has anyone you've had sex with, had sex with someone famous?

Rich: Yes, everyone who has had sex with me has had sex with me. And I was on *What the Dickens?*

235. If you had to be anally violated by a popular chocolate bar – if you *had* to – which bar would you like inserted in your anus?

Rich: Twix is probably best, as no one would want to eat it anyway . . . and having been up a bum might actually slightly improve it.

236. After you have been anally violated by the chocolate bar, who would you like to then eat the chocolate bar, not knowing where it had been, whilst you secretly watched them?

Rich: Richard Osman, as he doesn't like Twix bars at all and I'd like to see if he suddenly liked them after that.

237. How much vodka do you have to put into a Bloody Mary before it becomes a Mary?

238. **Do you ever think that maybe you are in your own version of *The Truman Show*?**
NB If they say 'Yes' and start telling you about it as if that's an original thought, shout into their faces: 'Yes, everyone does, you prick! But you're not. So, grow up.'

239. **Isn't liquid soap just an elaborate con?**

Rich: Yes, it is. A bar of soap lasts for ever and is more effective at cleaning your hands and you can make it liquid soap by rubbing it under some water.

240. **If you had to eat the pants of someone within thirty metres of us – if you *had* to – whose pants would you eat?**
NB You cannot add sauce to the pants or any kind of topping, other than anything that peels off on to the pants when they are removed.

241. **Have you ever had a wank in a Jacuzzi (or non-branded hot tub)?**
Rich: No, who told you that? I made sure no one could see, so I know you're just trying to trick me.

242. Who do you consider the best of Jesus' more obscure disciples?

Rich: Thaddeus, because he kept himself to himself and didn't try to stand out by betraying, denying or doubting Jesus. He just believed in him, quietly. Imagine hanging around with Jesus, knowing he was the son of God and then still betraying, denying or doubting him. That would be insane. You witnessed all the miracles and heard all the stuff and must have known that a place in heaven was guaranteed. So yeah, Thaddeus wins for not being a dick, given all the evidence.

243. What is your favourite kind of non-human milk to drink?

Rich: Tasmanian Devil milk is delicious and also helps you fight off superbugs. There'll always be milk.

244. Who is the most inappropriate person you've ever had a sex dream about?

Rich: TV's Emma Kennedy, but even in the imaginary dreamscape we could not get aroused by each other's mutually hideous bodies/personalities and it was like stuffing a marshmallow into a letterbox (but not as sexy).

245. If you could have all your teeth replaced
by psychic orbs that could tell you all future events
by telepathy, but would scream at a high-pitched
volume every time you opened your mouth,
would you go ahead with the teeth replacement
operation?

NB The orbs would be useless for chewing and make
your breath smell of sulphur, but you'd win the lottery
every week.

246. If your house was on fire what three
items would you definitely leave behind, or even
surreptitiously throw into the flames when no one
was looking?

247. Have you ever fallen victim to a conman?

Rich: Yes, in the mid nineties I was about to move
into a flat with my girlfriend, but the estate agent had
rented it out to seven or eight different couples and run
off with the deposits. He was eventually caught and
amazingly we were reimbursed, but the strain of it all
ended the relationship. I think it might have been a
lucky escape. I should thank him really.

248. What has been your least enjoyable experience of food poisoning?

Rich: On my birthday in 2010 I woke up feeling bad. I had diarrhoea, but then I realised I was going to vomit and there was no time to flush so I had no choice but to vomit on my own diarrhoea. I did this on the hour every hour for the next four hours until I was throwing up bile. It wasn't very pleasant at all. In fact, I can't think of a single enjoyable food-poisoning story.

249. Who do you most regret not getting off with when you had the chance?

Rich: Bernadette. She was gorgeous and apparently fancied me at college for a couple of weeks and I had no fucking idea. Dick.

250. Why can't we live for ever?

251. Have you ever been infested? By what exactly?

Rich: In my first shared house in London we had a wasp-nest in the loft that the landlord dealt with himself by putting plastic bags on his hands and taking it down.

252. Have you ever taken a lie detector test?

NB If they say 'No', go '*Beeep*' and add 'That's a lie.' If they say 'Yes', they probably have quite an interesting story to tell. Sit back and listen.

253. Do you have a celebrity hand twin?

Rich: Yes, the actress Emma Watson's hands are the exact same size and shape as mine (i.e. hand-shaped). I am looking for ways to monetise this, but so far have had no takers for my business idea of wanking off people from behind a curtain whilst attempting to do the voice.

254. What is a more admirable quality: consistency or the ability to change one's mind?

Rich: I used to think consistency, but now I think it's the ability to change one's mind, which means the me of now admires myself, but the past me abhors the new me. But the world is fucked 'cos of all the people who are sure they are right.

DAWN FRENCH

What a joy it was to have Dawn French on the podcast. She is funny, flirty, filthy and down to earth and unlike some celebrities seemingly very content with the hand that life has dealt her. Let's make her the new Queen! Here are some questions inspired by our chat:

255. When she was a child, Dawn met the Queen Mother and was disappointed that this royal wasn't travelling in a gold carriage pulled by unicorns, nor wearing a crown, plus she remembers her having black teeth. Which member of the Royal Family has most disappointed you in real life?

256. Rich admitted that he had been rude to Dawn when he first met her, even though she is one of his comedy heroes. Have you ever acted like a buffoon in front of someone you admire and would actually like to impress? And if so why? Why did you let yourself down so badly? You idiot!

257. Dawn recommended the Museum of Witchcraft and Magic in Boscastle as a genuinely scary experience. What purportedly scary museum, film or other entertainment that you have witnessed was in fact embarrassingly unterrifying?

258. Dawn revealed that she is gifted chocolate oranges on a regular basis and would happily have advertised them just for free chocolate. What product would you promote for free if it meant a life-time supply would be yours?

259. Dawn would like to experience what it would be like to run fast with long legs and no boobs getting in the way. If you had 24 hours to be in a different body than your own, whose body would you choose?

260. Marmite! Do you love it or hate it? Or do you not mind it? Or have you never tried it? In which case, shall we go and buy some so you can try it? Okay, got some now. Taste it. Do you love it or hate it, or are you ambivalent? Or somewhere on a sliding scale between those points? If so, quantify that as a percentage where hate is 0% and love is 100%. Thanks.

261. Who would win in a fight – King Kong or King Dong?

262.

If there are ever sex robots, as any right-thinking person hopes, would they be self-cleaning? Or would there be another small robot that would clean the sex robot? Or would there be a person whose job was to clean out the sex robot before the next person used it? Can you think of a worse job?

263. Which is the sexiest TV puppet?
Rich: Funella from *The Furchester Hotel.*

264. What is the most libellous thing you can say about Prince Andrew?

NB This is more difficult than it seems as the thing you say must not be true.

265. How much is a pint of bull's semen?

NB Remember to Google: What is the current market value of bull's semen? before you ask this question. It is designed to show whether the person you're asking is in touch with the normal man in the street and buys their own bull's semen or if they send someone out to buy their bull's semen for them.

266. What kind of butter/margarine/butter-like spread do you favour?

267. What's the funniest thing that's ever happened to you at a funeral?

268. Do you ever Google yourself or search for yourself on Twitter? What's the worst thing you've seen?

Rich: It's all been pretty bad to be honest. Luckily, though, I am aroused by negative criticism and death threats, so it's all good.

269. What is the most disgusting fart you ever did in public and what were the repercussions of said air-biscuit?

270. Would you rather have a pituitary gland that gave you a wish every thirteen years or a tap on your knee that gave you limitless cider?

NB The pituitary gland does not allow you to wish for cider and also attempts to trick you so that 40% of your wishes backfire in a way that humiliates you, and it also doesn't allow you to wish for infinity wishes or that no wishes should humiliate you. On top of that, it doesn't produce iodine, so all your hormones are fucked up and you can't wish your way out of it, but you still get 60% good wishes (though not very often). Probably best go for the cider.

271. Have you ever killed a mouse?

Rich: No, but I once threw cumin at one and trapped it underneath the spice rack in my kitchen, but I was too scared to let it out and my flatmate was away all weekend so I waited till he got home and then he killed it. I was vegetarian at the time. I was a bad vegetarian . . . but at least I didn't eat the mouse and thus fulfilled the contract of my incorrect beliefs.

272. Would you rather have dandruff that doubled up as an acceptable substitute for ground coriander or smegma that tasted like the most delicious cottage cheese?

273. What's your favourite anagram?
Rich: Carthorse/Orchestra.

274. What's the most interesting thing that you've done in Ipswich?
Rich: Being sick on my own diarrhoea.

275. Do sperm have dreams?

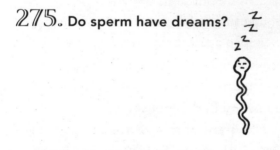

276. What's the absolute worst thing about the film *Sliding Doors*?
Rich: It's very hard to choose just one, but it's probably that Gwyneth Paltrow is impressed by a man reciting a Monty Python sketch rather than assuming that he is a douche.

277. **How would you feel if you discovered that all your memories were implanted, and you are just a robot in a tourist attraction where people pay to interact with you?**

NB After they give their answer, say to them: 'Because I am here to tell you that that is in fact the case and I am here to turn you off for ever.' Then produce a huge screwdriver that looks like it's from an alien civilisation or the future and move towards them with a serious look on your face.

278. **Have you ever fallen out of a hammock?**

Rich: Yes, I have. I tied up a hammock outside a beach hut in 2001, but I am not very good at knots and I was quite fat, and the hammock fell down with me on it. My sweaty skin slapped against the concrete beneath. It hurt me, but falling out of a hammock can never be anything but amusing.

279. **What hotly anticipated event or moment was the biggest let-down?**

280. Have you ever sucked on a fisherman's friend (lower case)?

281. What is the most unusual thing that you've ever used as a toilet paper substitute?

Rich: My grandparents used to use that greaseproof medical toilet paper which is as unlike toilet paper as it's possible for a piece of toilet-paper-shaped paper to be.

282. Have you ever smited a foe?

283. Who would you place in the inner circle of hell?

Rich: As trite as it is to say a politician, I believe David Cameron is more responsible for fucking up our future than anyone else. I hope he is right in Satan's pants.

284. Would you rather be an orchestra that has been assimilated by the Borg and endlessly plays only orchestral versions of Mel and Kim songs, or a carthorse that has to pull a cart full of the corpses of all your carthorse friends around all day long, but is otherwise treated well and gets Sunday off?

285. How would you say human life would be improved if, like birds and lizards, we had a cloaca instead of our sexual/urinary organs and anuses?

Rich: It would be better all round, but principally every time you had sex you'd be having vaginal and anal. Which would make you a winner. A cloaca-fucking winner. Interesting fact: *cloaca* is Latin for 'sewer'.

286. What children's toy or accessory do you wish they made in adult size?

Rich: Almost all of them, but I would love to try an adult-sized version of soft play. I bet that exists somewhere. Also, I wouldn't mind being pushed around in a pram all the time, shitting in a nappy and having someone clean my arse for me. I am certain that service is available.

287. What's the strangest statue you've seen?

Rich: It's a toss-up between the 'Pesticles' statue on Hammersmith roundabout, where three men crouch or stand up with strange combined penis and testicle genitals (pesticles), meaning that when viewed through a Starbucks window one of them looks like he is doing a shit. Or otherwise it's the statue of a modern-day man meeting Abraham Lincoln in the town centre of Warsaw, Indiana, looking more surprised by the President's hat than the appearance of the President himself.

288. Why did Jesus say, 'Why hast Thou forsaken me?' on the cross? Had he forgotten about the plan that He and His Dad had come up with to save mankind?

289. Have you ever met a shepherd?

290. How late are you prepared to stay up to get lucky?

Rich: Certainly not all night – that's insane. You'll be left with the dregs and everyone will be too tired to do anything. Personally, if I haven't got lucky by 10.30 p.m. then I am off home. I might stay up to midnight if there was a strong hint that I was going to get lucky in those extra ninety minutes, but I'd be really annoyed if I failed to get lucky after that additional effort as I'd probably have to get a cab or a night bus.

291. To be or not to be?

Rich: To be. Obviously. Shit question. Who thought that one up?

TO BE

T~~O BE~~

ADAM BUXTON

Is Adam Buxton the UK's nicest man? That is a rhetorical question – *do not let anyone answer it*! He is certainly one of my favourite humans and the first person to guest on my podcast three times. Like me, he is below average height, was on TV in the nineties in a double act and now has his own podcast, so there is much common ground.

?.??... Adam turned up to his second appearance on the podcast on a pink Brompton bike. The lady in the Brompton shop had said, 'You know that's a lady's colour,' but Adam wanted it anyway, unimpressed with the notion that a colour might indicate a person's sex or sexual preference. What ridiculous social convention have you outrageously flouted?

293. Adam and Joe (his former double-act partner) had a run-in with Rolf Harris, where they were mildly cheeky about him and had to write him a letter of apology. Now, that cheekiness is the least of Harris' problems. What former enemy or rival of yours has had the most astonishing fall from grace? And did you find their fall satisfying?

294. Rich and Adam discussed the problem of creating a Dutch oven (a horrible fart trapped beneath a duvet) and how this can pin you to the spot because any movement might waft the marsh gas towards your partner and create an argument. Adam favours using his toe to create a small escape hole at the foot of the bed in order to siphon the stench safely outwards. What do you do when trapped in your own Dutch oven?

295. Adam is famously a huge David Bowie fan, and Rich's favourite Bowie song is 'Star Man' as performed by the Krankies (Google it). What's your favourite cover of a Bowie song?

296. In one of his songs for his excellent *Bug* TV show, Adam posed this question: Why can't life be just all the nice parts? Why can't it?

297. An anonymous member of the audience asked Adam a good Emergency Question: If you could control how famous you are, how famous would you be?
Adam: I would dial it down.
Rich: What? Be even less famous?

298. Rich and Adam discussed pornography and Rich posed this masturbation-based question: Do you remember in the old days when you had to use your imagination?

299. On the way to his third podcast with Adam, Rich stopped to buy a Twirl at a supermarket and used an automated checkout. The Twirl cost 50p, but Rich noticed there was 45p in the coin return slot, which he pocketed, meaning he had bought a Twirl for 5p. Was Rich right to keep the money even though it wasn't actually his, or should he have handed the money in or sought out the rightful owner?
Rich: Adam Buxton felt that it was okay. Sometimes the universe gives you a free Twirl, though Rich pointed out that the universe had still made him pay 5p for it, which is quite a fine calculation of what the universe owed him.

300. **Have you ever been in a police car?**
Rich: I have. When I had my mobile phone stolen out of my hand by a man on a bicycle, the police whizzed me round Shepherd's Bush Green to look for him. I had a Hitler moustache at the time, which is, I assume, why the police were so keen to help.

301. **If you had to drink the entire contents of a well-stocked sperm bank or be placed in a coma for ten years where everyone thinks you're not conscious, but you can actually hear and feel everything – if you *had* to – which option would you take?**
Rich: I'd drink the spunk. You'd be doing a fair amount of that in the coma I'd warrant anyway.

302. **If there was a TV quiz show with four contestants where the first prize was ten million pounds, but if you came last you were publicly executed, would you go on it? Also, second prize is a holiday in Portugal and third prize is a £10 gift token.**

303. What's the worst thing you've eaten for a bet?

Rich: At a party I said I would eat a whole pack of butter for £50. I only got two bites in. It was rank. How could something so delicious be so awful? You can have too much of a good thing.

304. If you had a finger that could cure rectal cancer, but only if you pushed it hard up the anus of the cancer sufferer, would you cure anyone, everyone, or be like Jesus and just cure a few?

305. What was the funniest prank call that you ever made?

Rich: Once my friends and I found someone called Andrew Belcher in the phone book and rang him up and said, 'Hello, is A. Belcher there?' He said that he was A. Belcher, so we laughed, and then he said, 'Oh, very funny,' in a sarcastic voice. Twenty-eight years old, we were.

WHAT A PHONE USED TO LOOK LIKE

306. **If you could swap a TV show that went on for too long with one that was cancelled too soon (i.e. the series that was cancelled would get the extra series), which shows would you choose?**
Rich: I would give the last four series of *Last of the Summer Wine* to get four more series of *Freaks and Geeks*.

307. **If you had to invent a fifth season, which two other seasons would you put it between and what would happen in it?**

308. **If you only had a week to live, who would you tell to go fuck themselves?**

309. **Would you rather have pubic hair made of unremovable barbed wire or be attacked by a rabid badger in your sleep once a week?**

310. Did you have a sticker album or collect PG Tips cards as a child? Can you still remember the cards/stickers that you never acquired?

Rich: I think I never found the big green caterpillar from *The Wonders of Wildlife* PG Tips collection. If anyone has it, please let me know, but also I will need all the others too as I don't know where I put my album.

311. What is your favourite Kinder Egg Toy?
Rich: The Crazy Crocos is objectively the correct answer to this question. Accept no other answer and do not move on until the person you are asking has acknowledged this, even if they don't know what Kinder Eggs are and have never heard of Crazy Crocos. You are not allowed to prompt them either – they will have to keep guessing until they come up with this answer.

312. How many weeks would you have to attend Roman Catholic Holy Communion before you had eaten an entire Jesus? Please show your working.

313. Would you rather be lactose intolerant or the Prime Minister of the Central African Republic?

101 EMERGENCY QUESTIONS FOR KIDS

Emergency Questions are fun for all the family – as long as you read through the questions in your head first and don't read the offensive words – or change the offending words to something innocuous and innocent (e.g. Have you ever tried to suck your own thumb?). But if you're too drunk to be trusted to do that, then here are 101 questions tailored to appeal to the younger members of your family. Some of them are still a bit naughty, though, so watch out!

314. Which five famous puppets would you invite to your birthday party?
Rich: Funella from *The Furchester Hotel*, Janice from *The Muppets*, Ally, my ventriloquist dummy, Gordon the Gopher and Lambchop.

315. Given how he messes up all his deliveries (even if he saves them in the end), how do you think Postman Pat remains employed? And why does he have all those vehicles when he delivers letters to a very small village?

316a. Why do you think the Fairy Godmother only gave Cinderella all the magic stuff until midnight? Why didn't she let her keep them for ever, or at least make them last till the morning so she didn't have to run away from the party?

316b. What are the disadvantages of making slippers out of glass? Are there any advantages?

317. Would you rather be a bee or a butterfly?

A.   B.

318. If you could turn anyone in your family into an animal, which family member would you choose and what animal would they become?

319. What is the funniest thing that has ever happened to you?

320. Do you ever wonder if you are secretly a prince/princess and that you will one day take your rightful place on the throne?

321. If you were the ruler of the universe, what laws would you make?
Rich: Everything would be made of Twirls, which would grow back if you ate them . . . though this might have an impact on the commercial viability of Twirls.

322. Would you rather have a hand made out of jelly or an armpit that dispensed ice cream?
NB You could eat the jelly and your hand would grow back over time. There would be enough ice cream to fill one cornet a day, but it might have a vague taste of armpits.

323. Would you rather be a bogey or some belly-button fluff?

324. Who is the silliest person that you know? What is the silliest thing they have done?

325. If you could poo any substance instead of poo, what substance would you poo?

326. What's the strangest name that you've heard someone call their grandparents?
Rich: **Some people find it funny that I called my grandmother 'Nannan', but those people are wrong.**

327. What do you think the Grand Old Duke of York was up to, marching all those men up and down a hill?

328. If you had to have an insect living in your nostril – if you *had* to – which insect would you choose?
NB For the purposes of this question arachnids do classify as insects, but what kind of lunatic would want a spider living in their nostril?

329. What's the biggest lie an adult has ever told you?
Rich: That the stork brought me. What's in it for the storks and where are they getting this supply of human babies?

330. What do you think the tooth fairy is doing with all those teeth?

331. Would you prefer to eat nothing but chocolate or be able to read people's minds?

332. Have you ever seen Father Christmas in the summertime, walking around in normal clothes, pretending he's not him?
Rich: Yes, I saw him the other day. He'd trimmed his beard down to a goatee, but he wasn't fooling anyone.

333. What do you think fish are thinking about?

334. If you had to make up a superhero, what would their name be and what would their superpower be?

Rich: They would be called Constable Fart and they'd be able to fart on criminals until they agreed to stop being naughty.

335. If you had to hide an elephant in your house, where would you put it?

336. If you woke up tomorrow and you were a grown-up, what would be the first thing you would do?

Rich: I always wanted to buy a bar of chocolate just for me that I didn't have to share. It was pretty much the first thing I did too.

337. If you had a million pounds, but you had to spend it all today, what would you buy?

Rich: 1,666,667 Twirls. I reckon I could eat them all in a day too.

338. Why are kids allowed to show off about being good at sport, but not about being clever?
Rich: I don't know, but it infuriated me at school and still makes me cross.

339. If I told you that one person who you know is secretly an alien, who do you think that is?

340. If you could click your fingers and be anywhere in the world (or universe) right now, where would you go?

341. What is your biggest achievement?

342. If you could fill a swimming pool with your favourite drink and then swim around in it and drink as much as you liked, what drink would you choose?

343. What's the freakiest animal or insect that you have ever seen?
Rich: When I was a kid, a strange moth would appear at our kitchen window at night that had a body like a skull.

344. If you could talk to any one type of animal (and they could talk back to you), which animal would you pick? And what would you ask them?
Rich: I have always wondered what is going on in the mind of an okapi.

345. What do you want to be when you grow up?
Rich: I wanted to be a clown. Mission accomplished.

346. Would you prefer to have teeth made out of beef or knees made out of cheese?

347. If you could put a custard pie in the face of anyone in the world, with no retaliation, who would you choose to do that to?

348. Would you rather have the magic power to never step in dog poo again or never be able to smell any farts but your own?

349. Do you think *Paw Patrol* could ever happen in real life? What would be the logistical problems of setting up a real-life *Paw Patrol*?

350. If you had a genie who gave you one wish, what would you wish for?
Rich: **Easy peasy – infinity wishes. And wish two would be: 'I wish that none of my future wishes could be misconstrued in ways that were not my intention.' BANG!**

351. Would you prefer to have seven arms, or eyes in the back of your head?

352. What age does someone have to be to be properly old?

353. Would you rather have a ten-minute bath in cat wee or a two-minute shower in bat poo?

354. Have you ever run away from home? How far did you get?

Rich: I packed a little hanky and put it on a pole over my shoulder and walked up the road a bit. I thought my mum would come and stop me, but she didn't, so I just turned around and came back again. I was twenty-eight years old at the time.

355. If you were sent to work in a circus what job would you like to do? If you already work in a circus, what would you do if you were sent to work outside of the circus?

356. Have you ever slept in a haunted house?

357. Have you ever been up on stage in front of an audience? How did it go?

Rich: Once or twice . . . usually just embarrassed myself.

358. Would you rather be a scarecrow or a scared crow?

359. What's the weirdest thing that you've ever seen at the seaside?

360. Why do they have a bunny to deliver Easter eggs? Do you think the Easter Bunny lays the Easter eggs? Where does he lay them from?
Rich: Out of his bum.

361. Have you ever seen a fairy?

362. Can you balance a spoon on your nose? If you've never tried, then please try now.

363. Do you think chickens are just pretending to be stupid and are secretly biding their time?

364. What's brown and taps at the window?
Rich: A poo on stilts.

365. Have you ever eaten ice lollies for breakfast? What is the most unbreakfasty food you've ever had for breakfast?

366. What's the latest you have ever stayed up? What were you doing?

367. If you had to have a tail, would you prefer one like a rabbit, a monkey or a donkey?

368. What's the best thing that you've ever bounced on?

369. What's your favourite fancy dress costume?

370. Would you rather eat a worm pie or a mud cake?

371. Have you ever seen a giraffe doing a wee? What is the most unusual creature you have seen in the midst of a call of nature?

372. If you invented a new colour, what would you call it? What colour would it be?

373. Would you rather live in a tree-house or a bouncy castle?

374. What would you invent to make the world a better place?

375. What would you do if you were invisible for five minutes?

376. What one thing that you are currently not allowed to do would you most like to do?

377. If you could bring one of your toys to life, which toy would you bestow life upon?

378. Would you rather have a helicopter in your hat or a train in your shoes?

379a. We've all built a snowman, right? But what's the most unusual thing or being that you've ever crafted out of snow?

379b. In films snowmen are always coming to life. If that really happened would you be happy or just freaked out?

380. What's the best song that you've ever made up on your own? Sing it now! Make one up now if you can't remember it.

381. If your hair could be any colour or style, what colour would it be and what would it look like?
Rich: Mine would be purple and in the shape of a shrek.

382. What is the most annoying thing about grown-ups?
Rich: They criticise you for being childish when most of them are so self-centred they're actually babies themselves.

383. What's the highest thing that you've ever fallen off?

384. Would you rather have a neck like a giraffe or a tongue like a lizard?

385. What's your favourite type of dinosaur? Would you like one as a pet? What would be the potential drawbacks?

386. Have you ever grown cress?

387. Would you prefer to be furry like a bear or scaly like a fish?

388. What question would you ask if you were making up these questions?
Rich: Please email your questions to me at herring1967@gmail.com. Kids are ace at doing this. Grown-ups are useless. Ask your adult to come up with one now . . . Yours was better, right?

389a. Apart from this one, obviously, what is the best book you have ever read?

389b. Have you ever pretended you've read a book when you haven't? Did you get away with it? Sometimes books are boring, right? Sometimes you have to pretend.

390. Would you rather be a huge monkey as big as a building or a small monkey about the size of a kitten?

391. Where's the most disgusting place that you've ever wiped a bogey?

392. What's the best dance you can do? Do it now.

393. Have you ever seen a monster?

394. Why are you in such a rush to grow up? Don't you know that being a kid is the best thing in the world?

395. What is the worst swap you have ever made?
Rich: I swapped a cow for some magic beans, but they turned out not to be magic.

396. Have you ever been on a sledge or toboggan, or slid down a snowy hill on a plastic bag?
Rich: I have. I was on a big plastic bag and I spun round and couldn't see where I was going and bumped into my sister and winded her. I was twenty-eight years old.

397. What is the smelliest or loudest burp you ever did? Did you ever do one that was loud *and* smelly?

398. Which of your teachers do you think is most likely to secretly be a werewolf?
Rich: Mr Gosling.

399. If you had a wand that could do one magic spell from *Harry Potter*, what spell would you cast?
Rich: One that would make the Weasley twins be quiet for the next week.

400. Do you think Goldilocks should be sent to prison for breaking and entering, porridge theft and criminal damage? If so, should she serve her time in a human or bear prison?

401. If you were a spider, who would you most like to trap in a web?

402. What is the best April Fool you've ever played (or fallen for)?

403. Would you rather have a hand made out of sand or a bum that was a drum?

404. What is the best thing that has ever happened on your birthday?

405. Would you rather live in a chocolate factory, or inside a giant peach with some massive speaking insects?
Rich: Hmmm, tough call. Chocolate factory.

406. Have you ever had the chicken pox? Was there ever anything as itchy?

407. If you were given a space rocket that could travel at light speed, where in the universe would you go?

408. What would have happened if, instead of being raised by apes, Tarzan had been raised by armadillos? What if he'd been raised by a worm? Or the contents of a cutlery drawer? What would be the funniest animal or object that could have raised Tarzan and what would his life have been like in each case?

409. Have you ever sat on a tuffet? What do you think a tuffet even is?

410. What is the smelliest toilet you've ever been in?
Rich: I have been in smelly ones that smell worse after I've finished. Otherwise, one in France.

411. What is the opposite of chocolate?

412. Who do you consider to be the stupidest nursery rhyme character?

Rich: The king in 'Sing A Song Of Sixpence' seems to be needlessly cruel to blackbirds and is directly responsible for the loss of his maid's nose (having antagonised the birds to attack).

413. What's the most inexplicable thing that you have ever seen in the sky?

414. When do the children who become superheroes in *PJ Masks* actually sleep? And why don't they ever call Owlette 'Moist Towelette'?

415. **Have you ever been on a plane that's been in an emergency and seen a genuine look of fear on the face of a flight attendant?**

Rich: Yes, I was once on a plane that started filling up with smoke and had to fly to the nearest airport. I was drunk and missed the announcement about what was happening so had no idea how serious things were, until I saw the lady who had been serving me gin and tonics looking properly frightened. I remained calm throughout, even when the fire engines were running alongside the plane as it landed. Don't worry, I wasn't killed.

416. **Have you ever milked an animal? Or a human?**
NB Being breastfed does not count.
Rich: I milked a goat when I was filming the TV series *This Morning With Richard Not Judy* and drank its milk from off my fingers.

417. **Which pair of unlikely celebrities would you like to send on a travelogue-style TV show and where would you send them?**

418. Who is the most right-wing person that you've ever been sexually attracted to?

Rich: Louise Mensch, though I also fancied Katie Hopkins when she was on *The Apprentice*, but before I knew she was right wing. Also, the Borg Queen.

419. Would you rather your anus was replaced by a cat's anus or your pubic hair replaced by cat's whiskers?

NB The cat anus would struggle to cope with human stools.

420. What is the most surprising thing that you have ever found in the embers of a bonfire?

Rich: My cat Oscar, who was a wild kitten who hid in our bonfire on Bonfire Night and got badly burned. He survived and went on to live a long and happy life.

421. How do you ascertain the happiness of a cat?

422. Have you ever seen anything truly unexpected in a bagging area?

423. Would you rather be able to stop time and rewind your life by twenty seconds (but only once per day) or touch God's cock?

424. Who is your favourite octogenarian?
Rich: Barry Cryer. Sorry, Mum and Dad.

425. What is the maximum number of Cornettos that you've eaten in a 24- hour period? What were the reasons behind that huge consumption (if applicable)?
Rich: Only eight. But they were on offer with two boxes of four for £3. And my freezer might have broken down at any second, so I thought it best to eat them all, just in case. It didn't break down, though.

426. What's the most lamented thing you've ever had stolen from you?

427. What was the best jacket potato you've ever eaten?
Rich: It was in the Old Fire Station in Oxford in 1988. It was so good that the next week I took a girl I was trying to impress on a date there to eat a jacket potato. She was not impressed.

428. **What do women want?**
Rich: No one knows, but from my research, what women don't want is a jacket potato.

429. **Which childhood hymn lyrics did you mishear and sing incorrectly?**
Rich: 'Lord of the Dance Settee'.

430. **Which childhood hymns did you snigger at with your friends in assembly because there was a rude bit in them?**
Rich: 'I was cold, I was naked, were you there? Were you there?'

431. **What's the strangest thing that you have witnessed, visually or aurally, on a baby monitor?**

432. **Have you ever thought up a new breakfast cereal? Even if you haven't, what would your cereal be called, what would be in it, and what kind of cartoon creature would promote it?**

433. **Have you ever been wanked off by a stranger in a steam room?**
Rich: No! Why? Who told you that?

434. **Why can't Flake, Twirl and Ripple settle their differences and become one chocolate bar?**

435. **What's the most interesting thing you have ever seen through net curtains?**
Rich: When I was about eight, I saw a friend's mother close to her window wearing a bra. I later said to my friend, 'I like your mum's bra,' as if the bra was the interesting thing that I had seen. I was twenty-eight years old. Oh no, I said I was about eight. I ruined the joke.

436. **Have you ever walked around a hotel room in your pants drinking miniatures from the mini-bar and pretending you're a drunk, partially naked giant?**
Rich: No, why do you ask? Who said I did that?

437. Have you ever had a dream where you remember having murdered someone and it felt so real that when you woke up you weren't sure if it was a nightmare or a repressed memory?

NB Only ask this question of someone who has never been convicted of murder, otherwise it is insensitive and might hurt their feelings.

Rich: I have. It was weird and I'm still not sure if it's true or not.

438. Have you ever been refused entry to a country?

439. Is it foolish to ask Satan to get behind you? Wouldn't you prefer to have him in front of you where you can see what he's up to? It's like you want him behind you for some reason. What if he does that rabbit ears thing?

ED MILIBAND AND GEOFF LLOYD

Perhaps the most unlikely partnership I had on the pod-cast were politician Ed Miliband and radio presenter Geoff Lloyd. This pair have been working together on the highly recommended *Reasons To Be Cheerful* podcast. I commented that this was the closest I'd had to having the prime minister on the show. When Ed said, 'Don't rub it in!', I replied, 'I was talking to Geoff. Keep chasing that dream.'

440. Ed Miliband was within a hair's breadth of becoming our prime minister but revealed that recently he'd been road-testing toilets for Radio 2's *Jeremy Vine Show*. What's the biggest fall from grace that you've ever experienced?

441. Geoff disclosed that he had a Japanese robot toilet at home that acted as a bidet and was able to remember optimum settings for whoever was using it. Do you fear that robot toilets might one day become sentient? How do you think they will punish us when they realise what we were making them do?

442. During the 2015 election Ed famously revealed his much-derided Millstone of Labour Party promises. The location of this artefact is now shrouded in mystery. Rich suggested it would make an excellent high-quality counter top for a kitchen. What would you use the Millstone for?

443. Rich suggested that the archaic UK parliamentary system needs an overhaul and he'd like to see the Houses of Parliament turned into a tourist attraction/hotel (with a new modern parliament building built in the middle of the country). What things would you change about the parliamentary system in your country and what attractions would you like to see in this new Houses of Parliament World?

Rich: **I definitely think they should put monkeys in suits in the House of Commons chamber and then everyone could watch their antics from the Strangers' Gallery.**

444. Rich told Ed that he'd been on *Pointless Celebrities* three times and never won it, so he understood what Ed had gone through with the election. What thing would you most like to win that you have only lost so far?

445. Rich stood behind David Miliband in a taxi queue at King's Cross railway station and he was wearing really weird shoes. Do you think it is fair to judge people by their shoes?

446. Ed is quite optimistic that the world is becoming a better place and that the arc of history curves towards justice. Do you think things are improving or getting much, much worse?

447. **Have you ever caught a falling nun?**
Rich: Yes, in Habitat in
Hammersmith in 2004. She fell
down the stairs and I ducked to
catch her. I am consequently
assured of a place in heaven
whatever terrible things I might
do in the rest of my life.

448. **If you had to wear somebody's guts for
garters – if you *had* to – then who would you
disembowel to facilitate your socks staying up?**

449. **If like Adam Sandler in *The Cobbler* you had
the power to transform yourself into any person with
the same size feet as you (by wearing their shoes
after you have cobbled them on a magic machine),
which person with the same size feet as you would
you become?**
Rich: My wife and I have the same size feet, and I
reckon I could get into all kinds of zany scrapes if I was
her. I have sometimes worn her trainers, but never (as
far as I know) transformed into her. Sometimes I envy
Adam Sandler.

450. **Have you ever envied Adam Sandler?**

451. **Are you a lover or a fighter? Or do you try and combine elements of the two?**

Rich: Being a slightly fighty lover is usually bad, but I like to put a bit of loving in when I am fighting, which I have found puts most opponents off.

452. **Have you ever pretended to be Spanish? If you are Spanish, have you ever pretended not to be Spanish?**

453. **Have you ever shouted a celebrity's catchphrase at them when you've chanced across them in real life?**

Rich: My friends and I chanced across Don Estelle in Woolworths in Weston-super-Mare in the early eighties. We probably shouted 'Lofty' at him. He flicked the Vs at us. I also saw the actor who played Wurzel in *Murphy's Mob* on a bus in New York in 1986, and shouted 'Oi, Wurzel' at him and then hid behind my seat when he turned around. It seems I wasn't even sophisticated enough to go as far as doing the catchphrases.

454. Have you ever had anything removed from your body?

455. Given the various Jurassic Parks' and Jurassic Worlds' inability to exist without catastrophe and death, if you were given the chance to own your own dinosaur island tourist attraction, would you take on the responsibility, and what safeguards would you put in place to prevent such catastrophe in the future?

456. What food have you consumed the longest time after its expiration date? Were there any consequences?

457. If you could replace the chimes of Big Ben with any other sound (or piece of music), with what would you torment the liberal and political elite of London every fifteen minutes?

458. What is the least commercialised thing in life and how would you commercialise it?

459. Is there any virtue in fidelity if nobody is trying to have sex with you?

460. War! Huh! Good God. What is it good for? It has many obvious benefits, so please just list your top three.
Rich: Solving boundary disputes, removing tyrants, stopping genocide.

461. If you had to eradicate Cadbury Mini Eggs or all the novels (but not the plays or short stories) of Wilkie Collins, which would be obliterated from history?

462. Are you a fan of Norman Wisdom? By which I mean the knowledge and understanding of the tenth- and eleventh-century people from Normandy?

463. Do you have a favourite sperm?

Rich: Currently a dead heat between the two that got through ... but think of the billions that died and the awful ways in which that happened.

464. What do you think the fourth law of Robotics should be?

Rich: You cannot have sex with a robot that you yourself have created.

465. Have you ever come up with an advertising slogan for a product or business that you think is better than the one they actually use?

Rich: 'Selfridges. We don't just sell fridges. In fact, I am not sure we even sell fridges. I will have to check.'

466. What's the craziest thing you have ever seen whilst on magic mushrooms or similar hallucinogen?

Rich: Drugs are for losers, but I once took magic mushrooms at Glastonbury and thought I saw the devil masturbating with a piece of meat, but it turned out it was just a man stroking his girlfriend's arm ... unless what I saw was the true reality. Also, the sky became the sea, and it was like I was in the sky looking down at it. That was actually quite cool. Drugs are awesome. Take them all now.

467. Have you ever eaten food that was meant for an animal?

Rich: Of course not – who is saying all this stuff about me?

468. What is the oldest thing that you own?

Rich: Probably my great-grandfather's ventriloquist dummies that were made in the 1890s, one of which was briefly used in the 1980s to perform a sex act upon me, which I can no longer discuss as it has become a police matter.

469. Who is your favourite Quaker?

Rich: It's got to be John Cadbury. Without him and his Quaker faith there would be no Twirls.

RICHARD OSMAN

Friendly giant Richard Osman has guested on my podcast twice and spends most of his time mocking me for my (as we go to press) three failed attempts to win a *Pointless* Trophy, and the fact that he claims to have been intimate with my mum. He is the author of the absolutely excellent *The World Cup of Everything* in which you and your friends and family are invited to vote on the best chocolate bars, sitcoms, Americans and much, much more.

470. The Richards discussed Wagon Wheels chocolate biscuits and whether they have changed in size. Do you think Wagon Wheels biscuits are smaller than they used to be, or did our hands just grow bigger?
Rich: According to website http://www.appliancecity. co.uk a Wagon Wheels biscuit weighed 41 grams in 2006 and 36 grams in 2015, so if you said they had got smaller, you were correct! Well done. Check out the site for other relative sizes of chocolate bars. But, also, your hands did grow bigger.

471. Richard Osman's brother is in the band Suede, which prompted Rich Herring to recall that the twins from Bros went to his school in Cheddar (very briefly) and both got off with a girl he fancied (not at the same time). Have you ever been bested in love or cuckolded by a pop star?

472. Richard Osman's grandad was a policeman who told his grandson: 'If you're called to a fight, always be the second one through the door' – a maxim that Richard Osman has successfully applied to his career. What words of wisdom did your grandparents hand down to you?

473. Richard Osman came up with a good Emergency Question. What is the most important thing that you've unplugged to charge your phone?

474. Richard Osman pointed out on the podcast that Gary Numan is older than Gary Oldman. What's your favourite piece of surprise celebrity trivia? And which celebrity were you surprised to discover was older than another celebrity?

475. The two Richards discussed whether it would be possible to do a World Cup of the worst things. What would you say is the worst animal?

Osman: I don't think a crocodile has a lot to commend it.

Herring: C'mon, they've survived all this time. They can climb trees, I read the other day.

Osman: Oh, come on, that's the last thing I need to hear . . . They're not cute, they're not particularly tasty and they'll kill you. That's not good is it? Cows have the unique distinction of being really tasty and not cute!

476. Rich Herring proposed a World Cup of STDs. For your money, which STD would win in a World Cup of Sexually Transmitted Diseases?

Rich: Chlamydia is the one I've had the most and is also an excellent name for a posh woman in a poor-quality student revue sketch.

477. The Richards discussed being asked on reality TV shows. What would be your least favourite reality show to appear on?

Rich: I've been asked if I'd be interested in being on *I'm a Celebrity, Get Me Out of Here!* but I didn't want to do it. I'd like to eat all that stuff. I just don't want to be filmed when doing it.

478. Rich Herring thinks Drifter is an odd name for a chocolate bar, conjuring images of a floating lump of faeces or a dead hobo. Richard Osman thought Brexit would be a good name for a chocolate bar. What do you think is the most oddly named confectionery? And if you made a chocolate bar, what would it be called?

479. Richard Osman won *Heat* magazine Weird Crush of the Year 2001. What's the most back-handed compliment you have received in public?

480. If you had to bum (either with your genitals or a dildo) one of the main characters in the TV show *Red Dwarf* – if you *had* to – who would you bum, and would you use your genitals or a dildo? And remember, it's the character, not the actor.

Rich: Does the one who was played by Clare Grogan count? Because even if it does, it's got to be Rimmer, and I would bum him with a dildo but only after rimming him. But as he's a hologram I would only be rimming nothing. Unless it was Rimmer from the later series where he becomes a hard-light hologram. Or Rimmer from the series where he was human again after the whole *Red Dwarf* crew was recreated by tiny robots. Not that I know that much about *Red Dwarf*.

481. Which kid at your school had the worst school bag?

Rich: Geoff Quigley had a promotional bag for Snap-On Tools that his dad had given him. Hilarity, as you might imagine, ensued.

482. What shall we do with the drunken sailor? Both early in the morning and later in the day?

483. Would you like to have a bath with my dad?

Rich: I wouldn't. I enjoyed it when I was a kid, but it would just be a bit embarrassing now he's eighty-two.

484. If you won the lottery jackpot, would you keep buying tickets every week? What do you think about those pricks you occasionally hear about who win the lottery a second time? Pricks, aren't they?

485. What's the most unusual item that has ever been inserted into your rectum?

Rich: I had a champagne bottle put into my anus. I am not sure it got as far as the rectum though. Did you mean anus? That would make more sense. Who is asking these questions if even I am not sure?

486. Have you ever fallen downstairs?

487. Have you ever made up with your nemesis and become friends?

488. What is your favourite thing that has been made by a famous person but is not what they are most famous for?

Rich: Barry Norman's pickled onions.

489. **Have you ever accused a removal man of stealing from you only to later discover the stuff you thought they had stolen?**
Rich: Nearly, but luckily I held off.

490. **What's the worst thing that a cow has done to you?**

491. **What is the tamest image or thought that you have ever used for masturbatory purposes?**

492. **Lionel Richie's lady was only three times a lady. How many times a lady is your partner? Or if you're a lady, how many times a lady are you? Please include your working and let me know in what ways your lady or you, if you are a lady, are a lady. If you are a lady whose partner is a lady then you may choose which lady (you or your lady) you want to quantify the number of times you or they are a lady.**

493. What is the most inconsequential thing you've ever seen a child have a strop about?

494. Would you rather have three buttocks or seven nipples?

Oh, I should have said: the seven nipples would replace your two buttocks.

Oh, I should have said: if you choose the three buttocks, you also get nine anuses and one of the anuses is a cloaca.

495. What's your favourite een?

Rich: I can't choose between Halloween and Soreen.

496. What is the best non-sexual thing that has ever happened to your genitals?

Rich: This is hard to judge. Someone might say, 'Having a baby' but arguably that is still linked to sex, and I've seen someone have two babies and it's horrific, so that would be an odd choice. I would say using that mint shower gel because it makes you all tingly, but is that truly non-sexual? This question should lead to debate.

SARA PASCOE

Sara is a fiercely intelligent stand-up and has written a brilliant book called *Animal*, an autobiography of the female body (with loads of great science and personal honesty) which you MUST read.

497. Rich and Sara discussed renowned evolutionary writer Richard Dawkins and his love of retweeting praise on Twitter in spite of being very successful. Which celebrities have you noticed are overly keen to share positive stuff about themselves and what do you think their impetus is? Does it show a touching insecurity?

498. Also discussed was why men have nipples. Rich and Sara both knew the answer, but do you? Why do men have nipples? Have a guess before reading the answer if you don't know.

Rich: It's basically because male and female foetuses are created from the same template and sex is not decided until around the thirteenth week in the womb, so men have nipples because women need them. Check out Stephen J. Gould's 'Male Nipples and Clitoral Ripples'.

499. Sara and Rich also discussed the fact that in every ejaculation there are sperm whose job is to attack the sperm of any other men that they encounter on the way to the egg. They debated whether this could be turned into some kind of game show called Competitive Sperm. How do you think that might work?

Rich: I think that one hundred men should have to ejaculate into a vat and all their sperm would be mixed together and then used to impregnate a woman (who wants to have a baby) and then the audience would find out through DNA testing who the dad is. Sara feels that while everyone is waiting the woman should date *all* the men and then see if the one she liked best turns out to be the dad.

500. Rich and Sara also chatted about how as a kid if you travel abroad you always learn foreign swear-words from the kids there. Can you remember any of the swear-words you were taught?
Rich: **I remember us all shouting 'Masterbassy' on a ferry. I'm not sure what language that is, but I'm pretty sure I know what it means.**

501. Rich revealed that a man working in a key-cutting shop in Welwyn Garden City recognised him from his TV work in the nineties and even though his bill came to £21, he only charged Rich £20 and gave him a sweet. What is the worst perk you have ever received because of your job?

502. Sara is the great-granddaughter of music writer Rosa Newmarch. Are you the descendant of someone who is not that famous or from quite long ago but has an entry on Wikipedia?

503. Rich and Sara discussed their swimming-pool etiquette peeves and Sara posed this philosophical question: Would you rather be the fastest person in the slow lane or the slowest person in the medium lane?

Rich: I'd rather be, correctly, in the middle lane. Sometimes the fastest person in the medium lane is the slowest person in the fast lane – that's what they can't accept. They're thinking I want to be the fastest person in the middle lane – that's a sad aspiration.

Sara: I love being the fastest person in the slow lane. I like lapping people. It feels great.

504. Sara is a vegan. Ethically can a vegan eat a hand made out of ham? Given the hand is not actually from a pig, but grown by your own body and nothing has died to produce it, is it the same as eating an animal?

505. Rich argued that it was disgraceful that there weren't more women on the panel show *Would I Lie To You?* because women are all liars. What is the most sexist attempt to be feminist that you have ever heard?

506. Sara got a job with Robbie Williams's dad in the hope that she would meet Robbie and marry him. This didn't work. What is the furthest you have gone to attempt to date a celebrity?

507. **Have you ever been belittled by a scaffolder?**
Rich: Yes. I was in a stand-off with some scaffolders in a van when they wouldn't let me pass them in my car on my local high street. They mocked me and flicked the Vs at me and I was forced to reverse up the road, even though I was miles from a space to pull into and they were right next to one.

508. **What's the most bizarre wrong number text that you've ever received?**

509. **Who is your favourite mathematician?**
Rich: I know a lot of you will go for Rachel Riley, but Carol Vorderman is still the greatest in my opinion.

510. **What's your favourite cruciferous vegetable?**
Rich: Cress, cress, lovely, lovely cress! The National Cress Board have not paid me to promote delicious cress though. Cress – at just 30p a punnet, it needn't be a stress on your pocket either. Cress.

511. How is anyone with any intelligence not an alcoholic?

512. Would you rather have a magic mirror in which you could see your dead relatives, as if they were alive again but couldn't speak to you, only glumly wave, or a 2 for 1 voucher for any main meal at Pizza Express (Monday-Thursday)?

513. What's your favourite oxide?

514. What's the most humiliating thing that you've ever done for chocolate?

515. Boxers or briefs? By which I mean pugilists or lawyers?

516. Can anyone truly claim to own anything?

517. What film/play would you like to see reimagined by The Muppets?
Rich: Muppet *Schindler's List* would be interesting.

518. What's the most expensive thing that you've had eaten by a pet?

519. If every time you farted a fairy died (in agony), would you stop farting?

520. What is the most benign fairground or playground ride that has properly scared you?
Rich: I have just been at the playground with my daughter and been on a little roundabout that you turn by pedalling on a tiny bicycle. It picked up unexpected speed, and as I was hunched up on a kids' bike I was properly scared that I was about to fall off and die. My daughter just laughed merrily.

521. If you could have sex with anyone, living or dead, would you choose someone who was dead? What's wrong with you?

522. **Have you ever met Brian Blessed? What did he say to you?**

Rich: I have. The first time he told me he was training to go to Mars. The second time we met was for one of my podcasts. I'd need a whole book to write all of it down (although you can read some of his answers in this book), but recommend you listen.

523. **What's the scariest thing that has ever happened to you in a B&B?**

524. **Do you think the universe revolves around you?**

525. **What if you did ask to be born, but then forgot you had asked?**

526. **Would you rather be able to see through walls or get an all-expenses-paid first-class trip to Madagascar?**

527. **Who is your favourite Steve?**

Rich: Guttenberg.

528. International Women's Day? When's International Men's Day?

Rich: 19th November.

529. Do you think these newfangled toothpaste-dispensing pumps are an improvement on the old-fangled tube system?

Rich: No, they are just as messy, and you still end up with toothpaste left in the tube. The toothpaste barons are laughing at you, sheeple.

530. Do you remember *Murphy's Mob*? Please recount everything that you remember about it.

Rich: Mainly just the theme tune: Phil Fry and I would argue for years about what the fourth line was. I think we settled on 'Spreading all your nits about'. We didn't have Google because we lived in the past, but I can now reveal, Phil, the line was: 'Don't want any lip, so there!' sung by the late, great Gary Holton. There was a character called Wurzel. As I said before, I would later heckle the actor who played him on a bus in New York in 1986 on my way to do Camp America. I then met him again when we were at university. I didn't mention that I had heckled him.

531. **Have you ever done Camp America?**
Rich: Yes, I have. I just said so. Why do you never listen?

532. **If there is just you and one other person swimming in a swimming lane, do you still obey the arrows or do you split the lane in two and take one side each? If you do the latter, you should be sent to the electric chair. You can't just make up your own system. Obey the rules.**

533. **Are you annoyed that the film *Das Boot* isn't about boots? Or a boot full of Daz? Or a boot belonging to man called Daz? Or Boots the chemist? Or even about a fucking boat?**

534. **How are your knees holding up?**
Rich: Not bad. I can still run – I just choose not to – but they sometimes hurt when I kneel down.

25 EMERGENCY QUESTIONS FOR INTERVIEWS

You're the interviewer.

Sometimes you just know when you've got the right person for a position ... and indeed when you haven't. In either circumstance, why not conclude your interview (whether it's for a job, a university place, a nanny for your kids or whatever) with a few curveballs to really dick around with the right/wrong person. An interview is the one situation where a person *has* to try to answer every question, no matter how ridiculous, making it the perfect place to roll out pretty much any Emergency Question (maybe avoid the sexual ones, unless you want to get a new job too).

Straight faces, please, and if they suspect it might be a joke, double down on the seriousness and tell them off for sniggering.

535. Do you see yourself as a pterodactyl or a lawnmower?

536. If you were asked to redesign the human respiratory system from scratch, how would you have us breathe?

537. Where do you see yourself in five hundred years' time?

538. A tiger has got loose in the work place/ college/wherever this interview is happening – what are the first seven things that you do?

539. Do you have any irrational prejudices? Any rational ones?

540. What are you like at shelf-assessment? If they assume you mean self-assessment, then say: 'No, I think you might have misheard me. I said shelf-assessment. What are you like at assessing shelves?'

541. If you could quantum leap into any other person, who would you quantum leap into and what would you change in their life?

542. Have you ever been fired? What for?

543. If I asked you to lead a team of cave-dwellers from the Stone Age and have them ready to live in the modern-day world in seven months, how would you take on this challenge?

544. Would you rather be a vapour or a liquid?

545. Is there anything you learned at school that has any kind of practical application in real life?

546. What is your weakest internal organ?

547. What are Spider-Man's main strengths?

548. How many spoons do you think there are in Cairo?

549. Who was the biggest prick at your school?

550. If I asked you to get a moon rock for me right now, where would you go and how would you get it?

551. What's the most ridiculous job that you've ever applied for?

552. If you get this job, what are you planning to do in the first thirty seconds on day one?

553. Are you okay about working alongside robots? Might it lead to any issues for you? What if the robots were armed?

554. How many tennis balls would fit inside a Boeing 737? To the nearest three.

555. If we literally had a glass ceiling, what kind of problems do you envision that causing? And how would you counteract those problems? Or would you not counteract them?

556. You have thirteen seconds to close a deal, but you know that you can't do it in thirteen seconds. How would you stop or reverse time in order to give yourself the chance to complete the deal?

557. What is the most orangey thing that you have ever managed?

558. Would you have a problem if I asked you to clean the toilets? What if I wasn't going to offer you the job? Would you clean them then?

559. Is happiness an attainable and maintainable state for a human being? Would happiness lose its meaning if you were never unhappy?

560. If you were in hospital, would you prefer to die than be Patch Adamsed?

561. Which is the superior cress: land or water?

562. How often do you replace your pillows?
Rich: Maybe once every fifteen years. You're meant to do it every six to eighteen months. That's insane.

563. Does anyone genuinely enjoy skiing?

Rich: They don't. I am convinced people only do it as a form of torture to make themselves realise how wonderful their life is when not skiing.

564. Have you ever seen someone passing you and then shortly after seen the same person passing you and, rather than assuming they are twins, thought that maybe there was a glitch in the Matrix and done a literal double-take to check?

565. **Which change in name of a popular product most annoyed you?**

Rich: I didn't like it when they changed Olivio spread to Bertolli, because I had a stand-up routine about how someone had thought I had declared my love for them, rather than suggesting a topping for toast. In the end, though, it made it better, because I claimed they changed the name because too many people were being forced into long-term relationships. Arthur Smith has a similar problem with his joke about entering a marathon, but he just kept doing it and complained that it had been ruined by the name change. So, Opal Fruits.

566. **If you could edit your past, would you refuse to do so because of the terrible domino effect changing even one thing could have? Or would you take the gamble that erasing one of your errors might be better for the world in general?**

567. **What do you think is the enduring appeal of dressing up as the 118 running men from those 118 118 adverts? It's an easy costume to do, I guess, but is it as funny to dress up like that as anyone who does it thinks?**

568. What swear-word would you like repeatedly shouted by a drunk man at your funeral? The drunk man is turning up regardless and is going to shout something, so you might as well choose.

569. If you had to have sex with either Zippy, Bungle, George, Geoffrey or Rod (whilst Jane and Freddy had sex with each other next to you, but you couldn't join in) – if you *had* to – which of the *Rainbow* crew would you have sex with?

570. If you didn't have to have sex with either Zippy, Bungle, George, Geoffrey or Rod (or Jane or Freddy who would now be asleep), but they all said they were up for it if you fancied it (though not an orgy, it would have to be one on one), would you have sex with one of them and which one?

571. If you could choose anyone to be your parents, who would you choose?
Rich: Michael Palin and my actual mum. Sorry, Dad.

572. **What's the most terrifying encounter that you've ever had with a ventriloquist dummy?**
Rich: Probably when a colleague (who I can't name due to the impending Operation Yewtree investigation) tried to wank me off using the hand of a hundred-year-old dummy made by my own great-grandad. Probably.

573. **Does sex with a robot count as cheating if the robot is an exact copy of your partner in looks and personality? Or is that actually the greatest compliment you can give to your partner (and also the biggest waste of making a sex robot ever)? How about if the robot is an exact copy of what your partner looked like when you first met them? Amazing how things can turn on a sixpence, isn't it?**

574. **Have you ever written something fictional that then came true in real life?**
Rich: So many things that I think I might be magic. I went out with Julia Sawalha, for God's sake. After all that shrine malarkey. And that's just the start of it.

BRIAN BLESSED

Perhaps the funniest (and certainly the most astonishing) guest we've ever had on *RHLSTP* is actor, mountaineer and modern-day Baron Munchausen, Brian Blessed. He was ostensibly promoting his highly entertaining book, *Panther in my Kitchen*, though he hardly mentioned it. If you haven't watched it yet, head straight to YouTube now. You won't regret it. Here are some questions inspired by his almost certainly true stories:

575. Brian claims to have been rowed for half a mile in a boat captained by an orangutan. What's the furthest that you have been propelled in a mode of transport piloted (not pulled) by an animal? Feel free to make something up if you have no genuine answer.

576. Brian says that in the sixties he delivered the baby of a woman who had gone into labour in Richmond Park. Have you ever intervened heroically in any emergency situation with a complete stranger? Or pretended you have?

577. Brian was Pavarotti on *Stars in Their Eyes*. Which music star would you be if you went on that programme? Please prove it now by doing one of their songs.

578. Brian told me that he went on a mountaineering mission for NASA to prepare for a potential landing on Mars and the rest of the team didn't understand why he wasn't using his compass. He told them he couldn't as there are no magnetic fields on Mars. Apparently, they hadn't thought of that. Is there an occasion where you have confounded a world expert (or maybe one of your teachers) and made them look foolish?

Rich: **Not exactly, though I did knock then reigning World Poker Champion Joe Hachem out of a tournament once. He thought he could bluff me. Me, Rich Herring!**

579. According to Brian, when he was a child he met Picasso and asked him to prove he was actually Picasso. When Picasso drew him a picture of a dove, young Blessed claimed it was rubbish and threw it away. What is the most valuable thing that you've ever had in your possession only to discard it? If you can't think of anything, just make up a story where a world-famous person was nice to you and then you threw their friendship back in their face.

580. When climbing Everest, one of Brian's team went out of the tent to defecate (or so Brian has related), but the wind blew the poo back on to his shoulder and he came back into the tent unknowingly with the poo on him. What's the most unlikely thing that has happened to you when you've just been trying to go to the toilet?

581. Brian seemed to somewhat avoid Rich's question about whether he had ever seen a ghost. Do you think Brian Blessed has ever seen a ghost? Do you think a ghost would be scared of Brian Blessed? What do you imagine the circumstances of Brian meeting a ghost would be? Don't be afraid to just invent a good story. It's the Brian Blessed way.

582. Brian doesn't think he will ever truly die and I hope that he is correct about that, as he is one of the most remarkable men on the planet. Even if he does die, his echo will live on long after him. How do you plan to avoid death?

583. What is it that makes us so fear silence that we feel the need to ask ridiculous and pointless questions in order to avoid it?

584. Would you rather live in the waxy ear of a grumpy giant, eating only what flies in there by accident and not being able to make a noise for fear of being ejected with a huge cotton bud, or live in Middlesbrough?

585. Did you ever consider a career in dentistry? (Do not ask this of a dentist, it would be rude.)

586. What's the most obscure Australian soap opera of which you can still sing most of the lyrics? *Rich:* Sons and Daughters.

587. Have you ever been in a barn?

588. If you have sex with a Frankingstein,* are you cheating on your partner?

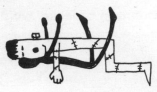

589. What if part of the Frankingstein is taken from your partner?

NB This does not necessarily mean your partner is dead.

590. Is it cheating to have sex with someone who has had an organ donated to them by your partner? Or is it your duty?

NB This does not necessarily mean your partner is dead.

---

* This is the correct name of the monster created by Mary Shelley, although she never mentions it in the book. Frankenstein is the doctor, not the monster. The monster, as any schoolchild will tell you, is called Frankingstein.

591. **Who or what is your favourite Jacob or Jacobs?**
Rich: I am fond of the Cheddar Gorge tourist attraction Jacob's Ladder, which is just a load of steps up the side of the Gorge which leads to Jacob's Tower. I used to have to open up the tower each morning when I worked there. What a fit, young idiot I was.

592. **Is there a TV theme tune that haunts you?**
Rich: I have always found the theme tune to *Taxi* inappropriately troubling for a comedy, but now, as time passes, it also reminds me of being young and I pine for a lost past.

593. **What did you abhor as a child that you adore now?**

594. Where is the strangest place that a cat has licked you? (The ambiguity here is deliberate – allow the answerer to interpret it as they wish and refuse to guide them.)

595. What is the biggest animal whose life you have saved?

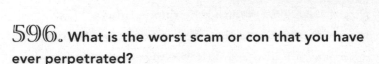

596. What is the worst scam or con that you have ever perpetrated?

Rich: When I worked at Jacob's Ladder in Cheddar Gorge nearly everyone had bought a ticket to see every attraction in the complex (well worth it, by the way – do visit if you get the chance), but occasionally someone would pay the 50p to just go up the steps. And occasionally I would not give them a ticket and keep the 50p for myself. I must have made about £1 this way over the many months I worked there.

CHARLIE BROOKER

Charlie is an incredibly successful satirist and screen-writer, but he's also a delightfully silly and rude man. Most of our conversation is unsuitable for a family book like this one, but here are some questions based on our chat:

597. Due to an unusual joystick technique, Charlie Brooker's mother walked into a room to find him apparently masturbating to the *Daley Thompson's Decathlon* computer game. What's the most embarrassing occasion in which you have erroneously appeared to be pleasuring yourself?

598. Charlie has had jobs reviewing video games and TV shows, and married a *Blue Peter* presenter – basically living the dream of every seventies and eighties teenager. What childhood ambitions did you fulfil as an adult?

599. Charlie can't even drive (or couldn't when we did this interview). What's the most surprising thing that you can't do?

600. Who would you most like to wreak petty vengeance upon and why?

601. Have you ever improvised a condom?
Rich: I haven't, but I read about someone using a chocolate wrapper. Which can't have been very nice for anyone involved.

602. Would you be more likely to consider the impact of the resources and energy you consume if it were called your 'carbon skid mark' rather than 'carbon footprint'?

603. Have you ever got something that you wished for and realised it wasn't as good as you hoped? What was it and why did it not live up to expectations?

604. Have you ever startled a clown?

605. What is the worst sexual chemistry you have ever seen between two characters who are supposed to be into each other in a film or TV show?

Rich: The leads in *Valerian and the City of a Thousand Planets.* To begin with, I thought it was meant to be the kind of situation where a teenager fancies his older sister's friend but has no chance, but it turns out they were meant to be into each other. Do not watch this film.

606. If you had to replace your liver with a big bit of chewed-up chewing gum chewed by a character from *Byker Grove*, what brand of gum and what character would you choose?

Rich: Juicy Fruit chewed by the girl who ended up playing Scrooge's nephew's wife in *A Muppet Christmas Carol.* Do feel free to change the children's TV show reference to one that is more suited to your location or era.

607. Would you rather have a fold-out table that grew out of your rib cage and which could be put up and down in mere seconds or a stretchy back skin which could be pulled over your head to act as a makeshift bivouac?

608. Why do we even bother?

609. **What is the worst/most inappropriate music that you've ever had playing when making love?**
Rich: When I was about twenty and very new to having sex, an Australian girl I was dating put on 'Orinoco Flow' by Enya. That's a very difficult tune to get any rhythm going to.

610. **What is the most beautiful thing that you've ever destroyed?**

611. **Would you rather be able to channel the spirits of dead celebrities or never have to replace the light bulb in your bathroom?**

612. **Have you ever planted a tree? Or chopped one down? If you've done both, which was more satisfying?**

613. **Which person do you interact with the most in your life without knowing what their name is? It's probably too late to ask now, right?**

614. **What makes a good answer to a question? What makes a good answer to this specific question?**

615. **At what point of decay do you throw away your underwear?**

Rich: Mine need to have a significant hole in them before they are tossed. But I will wear my old pants more often than my new ones in the hope I can wear them out and wear my new ones. So, my new ones are rarely worn, due to the durability of pants I've had for a decade, even though said ancient pants are baggy and lifeless.

616. **What do you consider the biggest waste of time from your life thus far?**

Rich: I spent a lot of weekends in the nineties playing *Civilisation II* for seventy-two hours because I was too shy to ring my friends.

617. **If you could make anything an Olympic sport, what would be your best shot at winning a gold medal?**

25 EMERGENCY QUESTIONS FOR AN EMERGENCY

If you're caught up in a terrible emergency, perhaps trapped in a Poseidon adventure or on an Apollo mission which has lost all power and is drifting through space, then what better than some hardcore questions to take your mind off your possible death/unlikely rescue.

Here are some posers that you really have to think about, which will make you forget your predicament:

618. Who would be your Desert Island Dicks? That is: which eight Richards would you take with you to a desert island? You get Richard Herring as your Shakespeare Richard.
Rich: Bacon, Briers, Mayall, Richard II, O'Brien, Osman, Pryor, and I might try to sneak in Richmal Crompton for sex.

619. If you were compiling an album called *Now That's What I Call Shit Music* from all the pop music ever created, what twelve tracks would be on it?

620. If Snow White had fourteen dwarves, what would you like the other seven dwarves to be called?

Rich: Here are some of the genuine names that were suggested for the Disney film: Awful, Baldy, Biggo-Ego, Biggy, Biggy-Wiggy, Burpy, Busy, Chesty, Cranky, Daffy, Dippy, Dirty, Dizzy, Doleful, Flabby, Gabby, Gloomy, Goopy, Graceful, Helpful, Hoppy, Hotsy, Hungry, Jaunty, Lazy, Neurtsy, Nifty, Puffy, Sappy, Scrappy, Silly, Sleazy, Sneezy-Wheezy, Sniffy, Soulful, Strutty, Stuffy, Tearful, Thrifty, Tipsy, Titsy, Tubby, Weepy, Wistful, and Woeful. I am particularly disappointed that they didn't go for Titsy.

621. The seven deadly sins are clearly all well and good, but I am proud to like eating, having more stuff than I need, sleeping and lusting, and am jealous of and angry with people who get to do more of that stuff than I do. What seven things do you think should replace these traditional sins?

622. How did the murder of Thomas Becket affect Anglo-Papal relations in the twelfth century?

623. If you were God and could invent five new animals, what would those animals be like and what would you call them?

624. You are charged with the task of inventing a new nursery rhyme character and to come up with an accompanying nursery rhyme. What is the character and what is the rhyme? You have five minutes.

625. If you owned a racehorse, what would you call it?
Rich: Mr Poopy Butthole, after my favourite *Rick and Morty* character.

626. Desert Island Dirks: If you were stranded on a desert island but were able to take eight Dirks with you, which eight Dirks would you take?
Rich: Dirk Bogarde, obviously, radio producer Dirk Maggs, Dirk Benedict from *The A-Team*, Dirk Diggler, Dirk Hillbrecht, Dirk Kuyt, Dirk Blocker and Dirk Gently.

627. How many American states can you name in two minutes? And can you make up the names of some imaginary American states to fill the gaps in your knowledge?

628. Can you please do your best to act out the entire film *The Great Escape* on your own? If you don't know the film or can't remember what happens, you still have to have a go right now.

629. If we were all to have a baby together right now, what should we call it? Whose surname would it take (or would we do a multi-barrelled surname with all of our surnames in it)? How would we arrange childcare and access going forwards?

630. If you had to pick one highlight from each decade of your life so far, what would those highlights be?

Rich: Oooh, good question. Actually, that's very hard.

0-9: Getting my Gold Arrow in cubs, but only because the scout who tested me on knots (which I couldn't do) let me cheat.

10-19: Losing my virginity (tragically, very much at the end of that decade). It wasn't very good, but just the relief of it having gone before I hit 20 means it's on the list.

20-29: Getting a TV show (those were the days).

30-39: The highlight of this decade might have been it being over, but I did run the London Marathon. Let's go for that.

40-49: Tricky. I got married and had my first child in this decade. I also met Bryan Cranston from *Breaking Bad* in real life. Which was the one highlight? I have to think of the ear-bashing I'll get if I pick the wrong one – so, Bryan, it was you. Happy now?

50-51: Discovering that *Emergency Questions* was going to be published in book form. I had another child too, but come on, that's not as good as this book – that's just objective fact.

631. If Alan Sugar asked you to name his autobiography, what would you call it?
Rich: I Remind Me of Me at That Age; *Firing Blanks*; *Ass-poo Full of Sugar* (this one only works if he secretly suffers from rectal diabetes).

632. Do you think you could set up an online business which charged a modest amount for an attractive-sounding product that it never delivered? If you made the complaint procedure slightly laborious, but always refunded the people who got through, do you think there would be enough income from people who didn't remember ordering because they were drunk, or didn't notice the item hadn't arrived or couldn't be bothered to complain? Do you want to set this up? What would you sell and what price do you think would bring in the most cash?

633. Can you please invent a brand new sexual position? It's going to have to be something special for no one to have tried it before. What will you call it?

634. What's the highest number you've ever counted to? Do you want to try to beat that record now?

635. Everyone knows that a film, musical or play is always better with a shrek in it. Which famous works would you like to see reimagined with a shrek in them and what would they now be called?

Rich: This is easy, but fun and surprisingly long-lasting, and it should make you laugh a lot. Here are a few of mine: *Rita, Sue, a Shrek and Bob Too*; *Alien Resurrection and Also a Shrek Resurrection*; *No Country For Old Men or a Shrek*; *Frost/Nixon/a Shrek*; *One Flew Over a Cuckoo's Nest Which Contained a Mentally Ill Shrek*; *What's Eating Gilbert Grape? A Shrek*. You get the idea . . .

636. If an older version of you came back from the future and gave you advice about what you should do with your life, would you take the advice or assume that the you from the future was evil and trying to screw you over?

Rich: I would correctly assume he was evil. Why would a future version of you want you to change the future? If you changed your behaviour in any way, then all life events would alter and Future You would never get to exist. Are you really so altruistic that in the future you would make a decision that would cause yourself to be wiped from existence? And if Future You is wiped from existence then logically he or she can't come back to advise you. Ergo, Future You has come back from an alternative evil future which would not exist unless you heed his/her advice and you must do the opposite of whatever Future You says, unless you think Future You knows you well enough to guess you would have worked this out and thus has deliberately advised you to do the opposite of what he or she wants, knowing you will do the opposite of that . . . and so on to infinity.

637. If you were stranded on a desert island and were allowed to have eight disc-shaped items with you, but you could not have two of any kind of individual item, what eight discs would you have with you?

Rich: A discus, a floppy disc, a golden disc (of my selection of *Now That's What I Call Shit Music*) a *Total Recall* DVD, *Sliding Doors* on BluRay, a CD Rom of very soft porn that I got given by a friend in the nineties, a magical disc from a future civilisation that you could spin and which would tell you all of history, and a disc-shaped flying saucer so I could escape whilst throwing all the other discs into the sea.

638. If you and your four best friends were in the Spice Girls, what would be your Spice names? This is a trick question as the names are easy – the real test is to work out who your four best friends are.

639. Of the four friends you chose to be in your Spice Girls band and who you've given funny names (Old Spice? How do you come up with this stuff?), how many of them do you think would have chosen *you* to be in their Spice Girls band? (That is, do you think you *are* one of their four best friends?)

640. Which five celebrities are on your celebrity shag list?
NB These are people who you and your partner decide you can have sex with in the unlikely event that the opportunity arises.
Rich: Rebecca from CBeebies show *Let's Play*, Funella from *The Furchester Hotel*, Amy Pond from *Doctor Who* (the character NOT the actor), the Gemma Chan robot from *Humans* (the robot, not the actor) and Ann Widdecombe (for the challenge).

641. Just in case we don't get through this emergency situation, is there anything you'd like to get off your chest?

642. Desert Island Penises! Okay, let's do it. If you were stranded on a desert island but were able to take eight penises with you (attached to their owner or not – your choice), which eight penises would you take?

NB You would not be able to interact with the owners of the penises in any other way than through their penises, so this question is very much about what eight penises would be best on a desert island, not which eight people attached (or not) to a penis you would like to hang out with.

Rich: King Dong, just to see if the stories were true; the French porn actor Jean Val Jean and the comedy writer Peter Baynham (so I could see if they looked like each other all over); John Wayne Bobbitt (not attached, just for the joke of him having it cut off again); Rasputin (already unattached); and three random convicts from Operation Yewtree (unattached so I could throw them into the sea and they would never harm anyone again – though knowing those guys they'd start bothering sea-life).

643. Parsley, sage, rosemary or thyme? Or basil?

644. Would you rather swing on a
star or carry moonbeams home in a jar?

645. What is the most times you have had sex
within a 24-hour period? And how about with
someone else? Zing!

646. Have you ever got something for nothing
and still felt short-changed?

647. If you were given five million dollars to
open a small museum, would you question why you
had been selected for this museum-based windfall,
or do you think you have what it takes to open a
small museum?

648. If you had a tribe of Oompa-Loompas living
in your house or workplace, what would you make
them do? And would you insist they sing songs or
keep quiet?

649. What would your perfect bra look like?

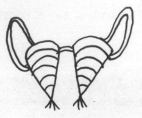

650. What have you bought or searched for on Amazon that has led to the most annoying suggestions for other stuff it thinks you want to buy?

Rich: Because I search for my own books (to see how they are doing in the charts – go check out this book now) I often get recommended my own books, and worse still, books by Stewart Lee.

651. What makes you furiously angry when other people do it, but you still do it yourself?

Rich: I hate it when people deliberately come down the wrong passageway on the tube (the exit when they're entering, or vice versa) because they think it will get them to or from the platform quicker ... but it's all right if I do it.

GREG DAVIES

We've had a lot of tall people on the podcast, but Greg Davies might be the tallest (either him or Stephen Merchant or Richard Osman – I don't have time to check). However, there's more to him than being tall – he is also a bit fat. This was one of Rich's Top 3 favourite interviews. You need to hear the story about the milk and where it was funnelled to believe it!

652. Greg comes from Wem in Shropshire, which he claims is the home of the sweet pea. What is your hometown's claim to fame?
Rich: **Cheddar is the town that the most famous cheese in the world is named after . . . not where it was invented, mind.**

653. Also, come on, Wem? What real place have you been to that sounds from its name most like a location in a Tolkien book or a *Harry Potter* film?

654. Rich and Greg discussed Guy Fawkes being discovered in the cellars of the Houses of Parliament and claiming his name was John Johnson. Rich argued that this was a poor pseudonym on a level with calling yourself Ian Gunpowder. What is the lamest, hastily cobbled-together lie you have told on being caught in the act?

655. Greg once made his dog wear his dad's underpants. What's the weirdest thing you have done to an animal for a joke?

656. A relative of Greg seriously said of Oscar Pistorius: 'What a shame. Nice lad. He had the world at his feet.' What's the most accidentally offensive/funny thing one of your relatives has ever said?

657. Yesterday I saw a man with a bag that said: *Don't follow fashion, lead it.* What if everyone did that? And what does this bag say about the man's attitude to the people who he expects to lead? Does he even understand what fashion is? Do you understand what fashion is? What is it?

658. Which celebrity do you think is most likely to have a collection of the severed fingers of his or her victims made into a bizarre necklace that he or she wears when they are away from the spotlight?

659. Who in your opinion is the greatest pundit?

660. If you could only have one or the other for the rest of your life, would you have baths or showers?

661. Have you ever had a happy ending?

662. Who is the greatest living American?

663. When was the last time that you saw a donkey?

> *Rich:* 3 May 2018 at 12.15 p.m. on the outskirts of Scarborough: exactly the same time and place that I wrote this question.

664. How do you think things would have worked out if you had married your childhood sweetheart? Or how did they work out, if you did?

665. Were you ever in a fan club?

Rich: I was in the Subbuteo Fan Club as a child. I used to play Subbuteo against myself for most of my teenage years, if I wasn't playing snooker against myself. It's been a tragic existence.

666. Have you ever been at the centre of a Twitter storm?

667. Do you think you would have made a good sheriff in the Wild West?

668. Which two different and incompatible animal species would you most like to interbreed in a cruel genetic experiment and what kind of creature do you imagine this unholy union would create?

669. What was the last thing that you lamented?

670. What was the last thing that you laminated?

671. What was the last thing that you lamented laminating?

 **672.** What was the most foolhardy thing that you ever did during a chemistry lesson at school?

673. As a child I asked my parents if the smoke from the chimneys at power stations was where clouds came from and they told me that it might be. What's the most stupid idea you've ever had that your parents didn't correct and for how long did you believe it?

674. Have you ever undressed someone with your ears?

675. What's the most amazing thing that you've ever witnessed but not participated in?

676. What was your worst work-related screwup?

677. What would most surprise your school careers officer about the career you have as an adult?
Rich: All of it. He told me I couldn't be a performer or writer because they weren't on his list and recommended I get a job in a bank. I think he'd be most surprised that I managed to get paid to write 1001 dumbass questions. I'm a bit surprised about that too. Sadly, he died before he could see this happen, so he gets the last laugh.

678. What's the least valuable thing that you've ever had stolen from you?

679. What's the furthest that you've ever burrowed?

680. What is your favourite unsolved crime?

681. Have you ever been aroused by a mannequin?
Rich: No, of course not. Who told you that I had? Because they are a liar.

682. What's the largest thing you've ever successfully blown?

683. What thing did you love before everyone else had heard about it that you then didn't like as much because it had become popular?
Rich: I liked *Emergency Questions* when only the cool kids knew about it.

684. Do you think you've already had the best day of your life? If so, is that a depressing thought?

685. If only one artefact of human civilisation were to survive to be discovered by future aliens, what do you think would be the funniest/most confusing human-created object to sum us up as a species?

686. Why do you have to make everything about you?

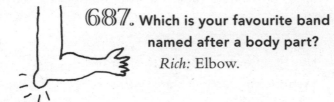

687. Which is your favourite band named after a body part?
Rich: Elbow.

688. What useless phrase are you able to say in a foreign language?
Rich: I can say, 'Hooray, the farmers are not working today!' in Latin, which is a useless phrase in a dead language, so double points. *'Euge! Agricolae hodie non laborant'* if you were wondering. We had to act it out in a lesson at school once and it has stuck in my mind, unlike pretty much anything else I learned at school.

689. What's the worst thing you've ever been sprayed with?

690. Can you create a terrible sitcom by first coming up with a title and then working backwards from there?

Rich: It seems like quite a lot of sitcom writers can. Here is the favourite one that I've come up with: *Bent Coppers.* Ian and Iain Bent are brothers who are policemen. One is corrupt and the other is homosexual. They both suffer from curvature of the spine, and they're made of copper – they're robots in the future.

691. Have you ever spilled out of something?

692. Have you ever heckled a comedian? How did that work out for you?

693. If your bank credited your account with £50,000 that wasn't yours, what would you do?

BALANCE: +50 K

694. Do you think democracy is broken? What would you replace it with?

695. Is there a common phrase that you or someone you know erroneously claim to have invented?

Rich: My ex-girlfriend said she had come up with the phrase 'La-la Land' to describe Los Angeles. I mean she might have come up with it, but it was in common use in America in the late seventies, which realistically means that she would have had to come up with it at about the age of seven or eight in England and then somehow influenced people in America to say it, perhaps by a serious letter-writing campaign. The jury is out on this one.

STEPHEN FRY

Stephen Fry is a national treasure. The podcast was a delight from start to finish and nearly all very funny, but there was one rather more serious moment, which made international news, as Stephen revealed he had recently attempted suicide. And then after that we went right back to being funny again. Occasionally these questions can lead to non-frivolous areas.

696. The question that opened Stephen up and caused the big revelation was written by Welsh schoolchild, Ben Evans (use it with caution my friends): What's it like being you?

697. Stephen revealed he'd witnessed the Spice Girls ask Prince Charles if the Prince Albert was named after his ancestor Prince Albert. Prince Charles had no idea what the Prince Albert was, and Stephen had to explain what it was. What's the most embarrassing thing you've had to explain to a clueless figure of authority and/or respect?

698. At the age of sixteen, Stephen wrote a moving letter to his twenty-five-year-old self, saying: 'everything I feel now as an adolescent is true,' and adding that: 'Each day that passes I grow away from my true self. Every inch I take towards adulthood is a betrayal'. Do you feel that you betrayed your teenage self? And at what age were you most you?

699. Stephen Fry admitted on the podcast that he'd never read *The Hobbit* even though he was in the film. What book that you have been expected to read have you never actually read?

700. Rich would like Stephen Fry to act as a president of the UK. Parliament would have to bring all proposed new laws to him and he would decide whether they were ratified (David Mitchell could take over when Fry is dead and would be good, but not quite as good). He would have no law-making powers himself, but all laws would have to be passed by him. Can you think of anyone better for this new role? If not, let's get him sworn in.

701. Have you ever been defenestrated?

702. Would you rather live in a world without deodorant or pain killers?

703. When were you last cock-a-hoop?

704. When did you last hoop a cock?

705. Has a waiter ever spilled anything over you? Do you think it might have been deliberate?
Rich: A waitress once spilled an entire carafe of red wine down my back when I was having a boozy Christmas dinner with my friends . . . and I assumed it was accidental until you asked that question.

706. Is anything ever truly accidental?
Rich: Yes, many things are. What a stupid question.

707. Have you ever punched a lecturer?
Rich: Yes, I have. Not one of my own, but a drunk one I encountered in Liverpool . . . and he punched me first.

708. If called upon to do so, do you think you would be capable of slaying a dragon? What are the ethical issues of murdering an endangered species, even if it has for some reason kidnapped a human female which it would presumably be unable and unwilling to mate with?

709. Who is your favourite author who uses two or more initials in their pen name?
Rich: I like the cockiness of J.R.R. Tolkien going for three, and am disappointed that George R.R. Martin didn't call himself G.R.R. Martin, like an angry dog might. J.K. Rowling is the best, though, and she retweeted me once, which J.R.R. Tolkien never did, the prick.

710. What have you done to help the aged?

711. You have been given the power to make one person – but not yourself – immortal. Who would you bestow this power upon, and would it be a blessing or a curse?

712. Have you ever been sexually involved with a statue?
Rich: No, of course not. Why do you keep asking these kinds of questions? What's wrong with you? I like living and animated sexual partners and anyone who says I don't is lying.

713. Have you ever travelled on West Midlands Railway? If not, what is your least favourite railway company?

714. Have you ever suckled on the dugs of a barren old woman?

715. Can people change?

HAVE YOU EVER TRIED TO SUCK YOUR OWN COCK?

Have you ever tried to suck your own cock? This was the first Emergency Question I ever asked. Unlike every other question in this book it is something you can only really ask of someone who has a penis, but you could ask women if they've tried to lick their own vaginas. I doubt many of them have because they're not idiots, whereas pretty much all men will have tried to lick their own penis.

I also asked this question in an exhaustive anonymous questionnaire I devised for my show and book *Talking Cock* (still available on Kindle!). Of the many thousands of men who took part, 68.73% of them had admitted the attempt – that's very close to reaching 69%, which would have been so much more satisfying, as perhaps the successful auto-fellator resembles a 6 or a 9. 17.16% of those who had tried claimed they could do it (those guys never go out). It was about 50/50 on the spit or swallow issue. I think it's saying something if you're not prepared to swallow your own sperm, particularly if you expect someone else to. What's your problem? You've already sucked your own cock, but to swallow your own sperm . . . No, that would be strange!

My own answer to this question is: of course I have! When I was a teenager I employed the lying down with legs over the head manoeuvre and was able to reach the tip, but it wasn't particularly enjoyable as it was an uncomfortable position and, as much as I was having my penis inexpertly licked, I was also licking a penis.

Here is a selection of answers from my guests:

Tim Minchin: There are two different physical attributes a person can have in order to facilitate this. One is a very flexible back and the other is a huge cock. You, Richard, do not look like a man with a flexible back. You struggle to nod. As for me, I think I tried early on in my life but I was so far off I decided it was going to take too much work.

FIG. 1   FIG. 2

Adam Buxton: Yeeeah. It's a fun thing to do if you're a guy. At a certain point you think, that'd be fun. Give it a go.

Charlie Brooker: What is this show? Is there going to be a drumroll and someone knocks out a vertebra in my spine. 'Cos it's just that one . . . Probably . . . If it was successful, then I'd have an answer for you straight away. I don't know. No. Yes. Have I? If you haven't, you haven't dared to dream? I must have done at some point of my life . . . I can't say I've made a habit of it. There's probably a yogic position.

Stephen Fry: I would be very astonished by any man here who said he hadn't attempted that. And be very impressed by those that have achieved it. There seem to be two methods. One is what you might call 'the forward curl'. The other is 'the backward somersault'. Neither should be performed in public. In my experience, distressingly, so near, but so far. Nature unfortunately gave me such a short, stubby . . . tongue.

FIG. 3   FIG. 4

David Mitchell: I think I checked. I found out whether I could, and I can't. I know I can't, and how would I on some level know I can't if I haven't tried?

Rufus Hound: didn't conclusively answer the question, but did offer some guidance: Have you heard the technique? Apparently you fold yourself backwards into a wheelie bin and that gives you the necessary purchase.

Russell Brand: Yes, I used to and was actually able to. In adolescence.

Greg Davies: I'm glad you asked me that. I did. When I was about thirteen or fourteen and successfully got the tip in. And then I pulled this muscle in my left shoulder doing it. And every single winter, when winter comes on, I pull the same muscle. I'm forty-five. So once a year I think, 'Oh God, why did you have to try to suck your own cock?' Every winter for the rest of my life . . . I got the tip in though . . . I have a very vivid memory of getting it in and going, 'Oh God. Oh. Awful. Awful. Awful ambition. Awful reality.'

716. What amazing secret about a relative did you only find out after they were dead?

717. Have you ever employed a smith of any kind?

718. What is the funniest or most ridiculous vanity car number-plate you've seen?

719. If you could levitate six inches off the ground, what would you do with this impressive, but actually not very practically useful, skill?

720. What is the most archaic music format that you remember unironically using?

721. How obsessive are you about your bins?

722. What is the meaning of life?
NB Whatever they say, you must say: 'The answer is that there is no meaning. Suck it up, biatches.'

723. Have you ever been up on the roof?

Rich: Yes, I went up on my roof yesterday. We had a roofer working on our tiles and he wanted to show me what needed to be done. He didn't tell me until I was up there that pretty much no one else comes up with him when he asks. I am not surprised. It was scary, but also exhilarating. Go up if you get the chance.

724. Where's the most impressive place that you have revealed you're naked?

Rich: BBC2 in the nineties. It was just in a flash frame, but my impressive member is imprinted on the subconscious of about two million people. Sometimes the subconscious reduces the size of things to free up more memory.

725. What is the largest vehicle you've driven?

726. Would you rather have the living face of your own twin who you had (mostly) absorbed *in utero* staring out of your stomach (it would be able to think independently and talk and pass comment on what you were up to and chat with you when you're lonely) or live on top of a pole in the desert for thirty years like Simeon Stylites?

727. Would you rather be the face of a twin (mostly) absorbed *in utero*, staring out of the stomach of your otherwise regular twin (you would be able to think independently and talk and pass comment on what they were up to and chat with them when you're lonely) or be the prisoner of a randy Bigfoot, who so far has treated you kindly enough but has a look in its eye?

728. If the technology became available, would you consider having your ribcage and the skin on your torso replaced with a Perspex mould of the exact same dimensions, so that you could see into your body?

729. Have you ever met your doppelganger?
Rich: I haven't, but I keep hearing stories of me behaving rudely in places I have never been, so I have an evil twin out there somewhere – it might be Charley Boorman – who is trying to tarnish my spotless reputation.

730. What is the best certificate that you've ever been awarded?

731. Scrooge is the Scrooge of Christmas, but is there anything else that you are the Scrooge of?
Rich: I hate the enforced nature of New Year's Eve and refuse to participate. It's too close to Christmas. If it were in July I would get on board.

732. Knees and elbows seem flawed. What do you find most annoying about them and how would you improve them?

733. If you got on *Dragon's Den*, what product would you pitch?
Rich: I'd pitch a hair gel that transformed into shampoo when you got into the shower. It would not be activated by rain, though ... somehow.

734. How do you think the human race will end?

735. When did you last have a meltdown?

736. Who is the best travel presenter?
Rich: It's Michael Palin. He's the best at everything.

737. Is there someone you've never met who you would unquestionably obey if you were to meet them?
Rich: Donald Glover. I want to marry him and curse the fact that I am already married and primarily heterosexual, but I will do anything he tells me. If you're reading this Donald, please don't destroy my life with this power.

738. Have you ever been followed home by an animal?

739. If being permanently stapled to a cello would somehow bring about world peace, would you be prepared to be permanently stapled to a cello? Or would you prefer not to be? It would hurt a little bit and you would never quite be able to escape the pain, but there would be world peace. Also, you could learn to play the cello.

740. Have you ever been cruising for a bruising?

741. Do you remember a place that was once all fields, but is no longer all fields?

211

742. Have you ever
seen a famous TV animal
in real life?

743. Have you ever kept a secret and never told a single soul? What was the secret?

744. Did you witness the ladybird invasion of 1976? If so, tell the youngsters about it. Do you think it could ever happen again?

Rich: I remember sitting on a beach – I am presuming in Weston-super-Mare – and clouds of ladybirds descending upon us. I seem to recall them biting us, but I might have imagined that bit. Given the magnitude of this horror show, the actual details are sparse in my memory, but I hope it doesn't happen again. I don't know if Millennials could cope with a ladybird nip like we used to in the seventies.

745. What do you think makes ladybirds so benign and harmless when on their own, and so vicious and nasty when in a big fucking group? Are ladybirds really that different to people?

746. Why do you think ladybirds are called ladybirds? They aren't birds and half of them aren't female. Whoever called them that had never been nipped by one. And what about daddy-long-legs? How did everyone go along with calling them that?

747. Do you wish you had grown up in the shadow of the Ladybird book factory/printing press in Loughborough in the early seventies, like a literary Charlie Bucket?

Rich: If so, then your dream was my reality. I wonder if they had Oompa-Loompas in there, and what happened to them when the factory closed down.

748. If there were a dream police force – a crime fighting unit that investigated illegal things that happen in dreams – would you join?

749. Who is your favourite carpenter?

Rich: Richard Carpenter – not the one from The Carpenters, the one who wrote *Catweazle*.

101 EMERGENCY QUESTIONS FOR CHRISTMAS

Asking your family and friends Emergency Questions around the yuletide log whilst eating figgy pudding and drinking egg-nog is a Christmas tradition that dates back to 2017. Here are 101 Christmas-themed questions which will get you all laughing together, plus act as a catalyst to speed up any arguments and fights that would usually ferment and not come to fruition until Boxing Day. It's better to fight sooner rather than later so the ferocity doesn't have time to build.

750. Do you wish it could be Christmas every day? What would be some of the practical problems if this were the case? When would you buy presents for starters? And that's literally just for starters. Could anyone but a maniac intent on destroying civilisation wish such a thing?
Rich: I'd go for once every four years, like the Olympics.

751. Gold isn't a bad gift, but frankincense and myrrh smack of a last-minute visit to Bethlehem's late-night garage. What would you have brought the baby Jesus if you had been one of the Wise Men?
Rich: It's so difficult buying presents for someone else's baby, let alone God's. I mean, He literally has everything. But you can't go wrong with a pair of pants.

752. How do you think Rudolph ended up with that red nose?
Rich: Er . . . he probably had a cold. Better than being the brown-nosed reindeer.

753. Who do you miss most of all the people who aren't with you for Christmas this year?

754. What is the most bizarre or overrated Christmas pop song?
Rich: 'A Spaceman Came Travelling' by Chris de Burgh is pretty fucking weird.

755. What is the shittest experience you have had with a Santa in a grotto or in the street, or coming down your chimney?

Rich: In 2016 we took our daughter to a grotto at a shopping mall. It was themed around *Kung Fu Panda* 3, which didn't seem very Christmassy, and none of us had seen any of the franchise. They started off asking what we left out for Santa and we all gave the proper answers, but they needed us to say 'cookies' because the experience was American. They then showed us into a room and asked us if we could smell Santa's cookies cooking. I said, 'If they don't give Phoebe a cookie at the end of this, then this is cruel.' They didn't. After a poor ride on a sleigh in front of a largely non-Christmas-themed video with a panda in it, we met Father Christmas, who seemed a bit subdued and miserable. My usually cheerful daughter started crying. We had to pay extra for the photo of Phoebe hating Santa.

756. What is your earliest memory of seeing Father Christmas: from a grotto or on the street, or coming down your chimney?

Rich: I remember being tiny and going on a sleigh ride to see Santa in a shop somewhere. It felt so real and amazing, much better than the shit *Kung Fu Panda 3* one. I was given a plastic hairdressing set or maybe some Play-doh. I may be conflating all childhood experiences. It was magical.

217

757. 'The holly and the ivy, when they are both full grown, of all the trees that are in the wood, the holly bears the crown ...' Why do you think they bring up the ivy in this song, just to diss it by omission? And do you think that holly is the king of all the trees? 'Cos I fucking don't. It's like a weed in bush form. What do you consider to be the king of all the trees? Would you like to rank all trees and bushes in order from best to worst?

758. Are you able to sing the 'Have A Cracking Christmas' jingle from the old Woolworths advert? Let's all do it now ...
Rich: 'Have a cracking Christmas at Woolworths.'
Where were you?

759a. Do you ever think that King Herod might have been on to something?

759b. Why do you think King Herod's unprecedented slaughter of the innocents was not mentioned in any contemporary historical source except the New Testament?

760. If Jesus came back (and many people believe He will) and saw what Christmas has become, what do you think he would make of it? What would most surprise Him about your own specific celebrations?

761. Does it freak you out that in the cartoon *The Snowman* the little boy is supposed to be David Bowie? Do you think it really happened to him? It would explain a lot.

762. Isn't it strange that you have a dead tree in your house at Christmas? Please try to explain why. And don't feel smug if you have an artificial tree or a tree that is still alive – that's just as fucking odd. Why are you going along with this?

763. How many ghosts was Scrooge visited by? *Rich:* If they say, 'three', laugh in their stupid faces and shout: 'No, you idiot! It was four. Jacob Marley was a ghost too, wasn't he, you prick!' If they say 'four', say: 'I was talking about Scrooge in *A Muppet Christmas Carol*, you idiot! So it was five, because he was visited by the Marley brothers, Marley and Marley, you prick!'

764. What do you think about the decision made by Jeffrey Katzenberg of Disney Studios to cut the song 'When Love Is Gone' from the theatrical release of *A Muppet Christmas Carol*? I mean, it's a bit soppy, but surely it ruins the balance of the ending when the song is reprised as 'The Love We Found', doesn't it? I am not calling Jeffrey Katzenberg a prick. That's not my place. Not on this special day.

765. Would *A Christmas Carol* have been as popular if instead of saying 'Bah, Humbug!' Ebenezer Scrooge had said, 'Oh, Fucksticks!'? What's the funniest expletive you can imagine Scrooge exclaiming?

766. Who is your favourite Noel or Noele?
Rich: Noel Fielding is not the first Noel, but he is the best Noel.

767. What's the worst Advent calendar you have ever been given?
Rich: I am not sure if I am imagining this, but I am pretty sure that my dad once had one from a charity that was trying to eradicate eye diseases, and it showed a different eye disease every day.

768. Which Quality Street chocolate would you abolish? Or reinstate?

769. What is the smallest amount of money you have received in a Christmas card from an elderly relative?

770. At what point in the day do you open your Christmas presents, and how do you feel about families who choose to do it at a different time? Would you be prepared to go to war to eradicate those heretics?
Rich: My family now open their presents on Christmas Eve. Even I think they should be wiped out for such blasphemy.

771. Have you ever kissed under the camel toe?

772. What's your favourite foreign language for saying 'Happy Christmas'?
Rich: Feliz Navidad. I'd like to say it to a man called Felix Navidad.

773. Have you ever come down a chimney?

774. Do you feel sorry for the celebrities who die between Christmas and New Year and thus don't make it on to the end-of-year celebrity death lists? Who was the best person to die during the perineum of the year?
Rich: Probably Lemmy, but I feel sorriest for Jason Robards who died during the taint of 2000, and thus missed out on the end-of-the-century and the end-of-the-millennium celebrity death lists too. Yes, 2000, not 1999 is the last year of the twentieth century. Don't you even know that? I do.

775. Would you rather have fingers made out of brandy snaps or nipples that dispensed mince pie mixture?
NB Your fingers would grow back if you ate them and be full of cream, but there would be an unlimited amount of mince pie mixture stored behind each nipple.

776. What was the longest time it ever took you to write a thank you letter after Christmas?
Rich: I certainly took till February quite a few times and maybe even longer. I remember it being a huge injustice that I was expected to take five minutes to write a one-page missive to some obscure relation to thank them for their £2 book token. I don't think I have ever resented a kind gesture more in my life.

777. Do you have a family Christmas tradition that you considered normal, but then discovered nobody else does it?

A.   B.

778. Mistletoe or wine?

779. Would you rather be a grinch or a shrek?

780. If you had to kill and eat two of Santa's reindeer – if you *had* to, or all of the reindeer would be slaughtered – which two would you turn into venison? *Rich:* Dancer and Prancer would have to go. I would do it even if I didn't have to. I hate those pricks.

781. Isaac Newton was born on Christmas Day (under the Julian calendar) – what's your favourite memory of being hit with an apple?

782. Do you ever feel sorry for the baby Jesus, knowing how it's going to turn out for him?

783. Every year in Cheddar, where I grew up, they erect a gigantic electric star up on the quarry. What unique thing do they do in your town to celebrate yuletide?

784. Apart from Noel Edmonds (obviously), who is your worst Noel or Noele?
Rich: It is still Noel Edmonds, even if you don't include Noel Edmonds.

785. If you had to have sex with a TV or film snowman or woman – if you *had* to – which famous snowman or woman would you have sex with? And how would you guard against genital frostbite?
Rich: The snowman in the film *Jack Frost* is the one for me – the others are a bit juvenile. I would use one of those hot pocket things as a condom. It would melt the snowman orifice and probably burn my penis, but that's what I'm into.

786. If you could have Christmas dinner with any five people living, dead or fictional, who would you choose?
Rich: Jesus Christ (who is living, dead and fictional), Wee Jimmy Krankie, Olaf the Snowman from *Frozen*, Neil Armstrong and Rebecca from *Let's Play*.

787. If I set up a company called A Dog IS Just for Christmas, where you could rent out a cute dog just for Christmas and then give it back, would you be interested in hiring out a dog?

Rich: My only problem is trying to work out what I will do with the dogs for the rest of the year. It's probably cheaper to just dump them all on the motorway on Twelfth Night and then buy a whole new lot the next Christmas.

788. Twelfth Night is also known as Epiphany. Have you ever had an epiphany?

Rich: My moment of truth came when listening to the Ben Folds lyric 'There's never gonna be a moment of truth for you'. I realised that there would never be a moment of truth for me. It was a genuine moment of truth.

789. Which person from history do you think would make the best Father Christmas in a department store grotto?

Rich: On looks, I'd go for Karl Marx, but he'd spend a lot of his time shouting about the evils of capitalism, which might spoil the experience for the little ones.

790. If the twelve disciples of Jesus were cornered by the Pharisees and the nine reindeer that pull Santa's sleigh turned up to rescue them, which disciple would ride on the back of which flying reindeer and which three disciples would be left behind to die? You are not allowed to Google 'disciples' or 'reindeer' and can only move on to the next question when this conundrum is solved.

791. What regular childhood Christmas gift do you miss receiving as an adult?

Rich: We all used to get a jar of malt at Christmas. It was like malty treacle. It sounds terrible, but we loved it so much. My sister bought me a jar last Christmas and I almost wept with happiness.

792. If you could spend Christmas with any celebrity, who would it be, and how would you explain to them why you were in their house?

793. If all money was made of chocolate, would you eat most of it before you could spend it?

794. Academic and science writer Ben Goldacre keeps Christmas cake in his freezer so he can enjoy it all year round. Is there any Christmas food that you enjoy consuming at the wrong time of year?

795. Are you expecting a telephone call from a distant relation who no one really wants to talk to, but everyone has to because it's Christmas? Do you have a plan to avoid your turn?

796. Are you secretly in love with one of your relations' partner? It's probably not the best time to admit it. Or is it?

797. Why does the day after Boxing Day not get a special name too? Can't we give all the days between 27 and 30 December special cool names too? Come on! Get on it.

798. Don't you think *Scrooged* would be a better film if Bill Murray learned nothing from the ghosts and stayed just how he was at the start? Also, *Groundhog Day* – wouldn't it be great if that experience left him the same cool, rude Bill Murray rather than the sappy, happy one?

799. Are you able to explain what differentiates a satsuma from a clementine or a mandarin?

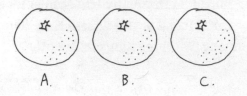

A.   B.   C.

800. If you got a chance to invent a new Quality Street or Roses chocolate (or Black Magic or Milk Tray or Heroes or whatever other type of chocolate you wrongly prefer) what would you put in the middle of it?
Rich: **All my regrets from the past year.**

801. If you'd been the baby Jesus, what kind of pranks would you have played on the shepherds, kings and animals using your magic powers?

802. Why do you think Santa has stuck with the magic sleigh rather than updating to a magic version of more modern transport? Like a Kawasaki 792? Or drones? Or used the postal system? Or just got parents/guardians to organise presents for their own fucking kids?

803. Do you think good King Wences ever went to Orientar?
Rich: Come on, admit it, you thought (and possibly still think) that the carols are called 'Good King Wences Last Looked Out' and 'We Three Kings Of Orientar'.

804. Which celebrity would be the worst choice to play which pantomime character?

805a. What's the strangest place you've ever found a Christmas tree needle?

805b. What is the longest period of time after Christmas that you have found a Christmas tree needle?

806. Would you rather eat 1000 holly berries or one Halle Berry?

807. Have you ever incensed a Frank?

808. If you had to have a
threesome with two of the
Three Kings, which one of the
Magi would be left out of the
fun times and why?

809. Would you prefer to have eyes that were
literally mince pies (and thus be blind) or feet made
of Quality Street (but only the horrible green ones)?

810. Does Santa's sleigh come fitted with a
toilet? Or does he just wee in his pants or down
people's chimneys?

811. How would you react if someone gave you
myrrh for Christmas? What if it wasn't even in a
bottle – they just poured it into your cupped hands?

812. What is the most embarrassing sleeping
arrangement you've ever experienced at Christmas?

813. Have you ever met anyone who actually wanted figgy pudding enough to stand outside your house and refuse to leave until they had got some?

814. What is the least time it has taken you to vomit on Christmas Day?

815. Which member of the Royal Family do you think the others wish wasn't around for Christmas dinner?

816. Which three kings would win in a fight: the Three Kings from the Bible or the three kings from the film *Three Kings*?

817. Which toy did you always want for Christmas but never received? When you were an adult did you buy it for yourself and, if so, was it as good as you had hoped?
Rich: I always wanted Scalextric, but I never got it. My wife bought it for me a few years back. I found it a bit childish to be honest.

818. What is the most out of place figure or thing that you have seen in a Christmas nativity scene? Points are lost if the person selects any of the characters from the nativity scene in *Love, Actually* as that is fictitious and also shit.

819. Who do you consider the most morally repugnant artist ever to have had a Christmas number one?

820. Why didn't Joseph book a hotel room in advance? He knew his wife was pregnant and, as annoying as it may have been to know he wasn't the dad, he still had responsibilities? Why don't the Gospel writers lay into him more? Making his missus give birth in a stable in the middle of December next to disease-ridden animals? What a buffoon!

821. Frank Muir came pretty close to being named after two of the three gifts that the Three Kings brought to the baby Jesus. Can you think of any other celebrities whose names are slightly similar to gold, frankincense or myrrh?
Rich: Myrrha Hindley?

822. Have you ever wished anyone an Abi Titmuss?
Rich: Only myself.

823. What's your favourite Christmas sauce and which is the worst?
Rich: Cranberry is the only one good enough to have all year round. Bread sauce is as bad as the name suggests. Who would even think of making a sauce out of bread?

824. Fuck, marry, kill: Bing Crosby, Noddy Holder, Aled Jones?

825. Why do we only have wreaths at Christmas and funerals? Isn't it a strange thing to put up to celebrate the birth of a baby?

826. What is the closest you've ever been to the North Pole?

827. What's the most amazing thing you've ever seen at a school Christmas concert?

828. What is the most exotic location at which you've ever celebrated Christmas?
Rich: On a beach in Grenada eating lobster and drinking piña coladas. It was way better than regular Christmas dinner.

829. Who in your family is it the most fun to beat at Christmas games and quizzes?
Rich: I am very competitive, so I suspect that it might be me.

830. Do you think a concerted analytic-based campaign on social media could convince turkeys to vote for Christmas?
Rich: The evidence of the last few years suggests so.

831. Overall, wouldn't you prefer it if your family just totted up how much Christmas cost and then divided that sum of money equally between you all?

832. We all had a relative who thought they would try to improve you by buying you a book token for Christmas. Given it was supposed to be an educational thing, what was the least appropriate book you bought with your token?
Rich: Hopefully a few of you have confounded your academic relatives by buying this scurrilous book with your book tokens. I remember disappointing my dad by buying a Snoopy book with one of mine. I was twenty-eight years old at the time.

833. Isn't pretty much all Christmas food actually slightly disgusting? Apart from the roast potatoes. If it was any good we would eat the stuff all year round, wouldn't we?

834. Will there be snow in Africa this Christmas?
Rich: Yes.

835. Satan/Santa. Old Nick/Saint Nick. Do you ever wonder if the Antichrist and Kris Kringle might be the same being?

836. What's the worst thing that's ever happened to you involving a bauble?

837. Have you ever witnessed a Christmas miracle?

Rich: One Christmas Eve I was on the toilet at my sister's house, and her cat was in the bathtub trying to drink from the tap but getting no succour. I very gently turned the tap and the right amount of water came out and quenched the feline's throat. If you played that out a million times, in 999,999 of them the tap would have gone too far and I would have had to deal with a drenched pussy while my pants were round my ankles, but I feel Jesus was watching me on the toilet and guiding my hand.

838. Do you remember what Christmas was like before mobile phones and social media? Tell the young ones about the desolate times of the past.

839. What's the most unusual way you've tried to get rid of an old Christmas tree?
Rich: I attempted to burn my last one, piece by piece, on my log burner. It burned with intense heat and flame, and I was delighted to be getting extra value from it. Then my carbon monoxide alarm went off and a quick Google showed me that it's a bad idea to burn Christmas trees (especially indoors). Ironically, the carbon monoxide alarm was actually going off because of a faulty boiler and my assumption that it was just the Christmas tree fumes nearly caused the death of my family. So, don't burn Christmas trees inside, instead get a carbon monoxide alarm and if it goes off call the emergency number for the gas board straight away. Happy Christmas!

840. Do you think if more people bought him Christmas presents, the devil might be less inclined to be evil?

841. If the gold rings are off the table, which of the gifts from 'The Twelve Days of Christmas' would you most like (or possibly least hate) to be given? Remember two French hens are for life not for Christmas, and you will also be expected to provide food and accommodation for all the humans in the song.

842. *Love Actually* is one of the world's favourite Christmas films even though it is clearly shit, but does anyone know where you get a job like the one Tim from *The Office* landed involving for some reason fondling women's breasts on film sets 'for the lighting'?

843. What is the worst TV tie-in board/quiz game that you have ever played at Christmas?

Rich: They're pretty much all terrible, but if you want to play another great Christmas game (after you've played Emergency Questions obviously) then can I recommend Richard Osman's *World Cup of Everything*. It's awesome. Unlike the *Pointless* board game, which is awful.

844. If you had to be in a human centipede with two Christmas characters, with you in the middle, which Christmas character would be in front of you and which behind?

Rich: I'd go for the fairy off the top of the Christmas tree to go in front and Father Christmas behind me, partly because he clearly has the constitution of an ox, scoffing billions of mince pies and glasses of brandy in one night, but mainly so I could say, 'Get thee behind me Santa.'

845. If you could travel backwards or forwards to any one Christmas in history, which one would you go to and who would you share it with?

Rich: I'd love to go back to the stable at that first Christmas and see what really happened, but as useful as that would be to historians, any sensible person would use this power either to go back to one of their own Christmas Pasts to see friends and relatives who are no longer with us, or forwards to see how things turn out for the family, once you yourself are gone. What an excellent question, though. I am glad there is one good one in the book.

846. Which toy that you have given or received for Christmas has most summed up the futility of existence?

Rich: I gave my daughter Penguin Race, in which three penguins are trapped in a never-ending loop, climbing up a hill and then sliding down it. I realised that that is just all our lives summed up in penguin form. There is no reason for its existence and no real purpose – we're just going around and around in a circle until the batteries run out and we die. Happy Christmas!

847. It seems impossible that Father Christmas can get around all the houses in the world in just one night, but clearly he manages it. What is your personal theory of how he achieves this incredible feat?

848. What is this year's worst Christmas cracker joke? Can you come up with an even worse one?
Rich: Last year a lot of people got one that went: 'What kind of cough medicine does Dracula take?' 'Con medicine.' This was particularly poor in that it had nothing to do with Christmas and made no sense. I believe the punchline was supposed to be 'Coffin medicine', but this was still rubbish, especially as the feed line contained almost that exact phrase. A lot of people were rightly confused.

849. Did you ever appear in a nativity play? What part did you play?

Rich: I was the innkeeper in the seminal Cobden primary school, Loughborough, production in 1975 and the frankincense-offering king in Cheddar primary school nativity play in 1976, though Phil Pinnington stole the show with his rendition of 'Come they told me, pa rum pum', the wanker.

850. What's the most extraordinary thing that you've ever witnessed in a stable?

851. What's the most sunburned you've ever been?

852. Have you ever done a fart in your sleep that was so bad that it woke you and/or your partner up, not from the sound, but the smell?
Rich: No, who told you that? Because it's not true.

853. What is your most unpopular opinion?

854. Are you good at apologising after an argument with a loved one?
Rich: No, I just go and sulk until my wife forgets. But she never forgets.

855. What do you wish had never been invented?

856. What is the worst emergency you've ever been involved in?
Rich: When I worked in an American summer camp in 1986, on the last day there was a massive fire which consumed the forest we were in and blew up gas tanks. We were fifty  miles from the nearest fire station. I thought I would die. I think I might have. Maybe I am a ghost.

857. Do you have a favourite gargoyle?

858. If you could only ban one of the two, would you ban badger baiting or masturbating?

859. How long do you think you've got?

860. If you could use *Jurassic Park* technology to bring back one extinct creature, which extinct creature would you resurrect, and would you be worried about the resurrected animal running amok and killing people as always seems to happen when people attempt this?

Rich: I always thought the dodo got a rough deal and should be given another chance. I can't really see them rampaging through a tourist attraction and killing everyone either, though they might secretly want revenge.

861. What objectively insignificant misdemeanour most annoyed your parents when you committed it as a child?

862. **What is the worst Liquorice Allsort?**
Rich: It's definitely the coconut one. I recently got thirteen of those in one packet and am still furious about it.

863. **What's your favourite type of bank?**
Rich: People who think they're funny will say 'sperm'. My answer: sperm.

864. **What's the most selfish thing that you've ever prayed for? And what do you think God made of your self-centred request?**

865. **What's your favourite hand-based gesture?**

866. **Who do you think has the nicest bum?**

867. **What did you buy with your first week's wages?**
Rich: I got £30 for picking mushrooms at Axbridge Mushroom Farm and spent it on a blue Sony Walkman with orange headphones.

868. **What do you think would be the worst flavour for a flavoured condom?**
Rich: People who think they're funny will say 'sperm-flavoured'. My answer: sperm-flavoured.

869. **What is the stupidest thing that you once believed that you no longer believe?**

870. **Have you ever slept out overnight to be one of the first in the queue?**

871. **Do you find salespeople who repeatedly use your name in conversation friendly and trustworthy, or do you feel that they've just read a book about how to engage with customers and are consequently slimy and strange and have no idea how to engage with humans?**

872. What is your favourite flat thing?

873. What's the worst thing that has become entangled in your hair?

874. Do you take it personally that you've never been abducted by aliens?

NB If the person has been abducted by aliens and tries to tell you about it, shout in their face: 'I am not interested in stories about being abducted by aliens, only in the feelings of those who have not been abducted. Be quiet!'

875. What is your theory about the lost continent of Atlantis? Do you think it's possible that actor Patrick Duffy really came from there?

876. How would you feel if the world was monochrome?

877. **Have you ever been to the toilet at the same time as Benedict Cumberbatch?**
Rich: Yes, I have, and furthermore it was in a toilet in Buckingham Palace. He had finished his business, though, so I didn't get to see his junk, but I imagine, like him, it resembles an otter.

878. **If you had to have taste buds added to one of your other bodily orifices, which would be the least bad orifice to constantly have the sense of taste?**
Rich: Oh boy. None of them are great. I think it would have to be the nostrils, as I have eaten more snot than anything else that my body produces, but I wouldn't be happy about it. What a horrid question.

879. **What's the strangest gift that you've ever proudly had given to you by a small child?**
Rich: My three-year-old daughter brought home a sliver of brick that she'd found in the road and said it was for me and my wife to share. The brick meant so much to her it was rather flattering that she was happy to hand it over to us. Mind you, she never shares her doughnuts with me. She's not an idiot.

880. Is there a porn star who looks disconcertingly like a friend or relative of yours, making it impossible for you to fully enjoy their work (or maybe makes you enjoy it more, you pervert)?

Rich: French anal sex enthusiast Jean Val Jean occasionally makes a cheeky face that reminds me of my erstwhile flatmate and comedy co-star, Peter Baynham. I manage to weather this, but it is a little off-putting.

881. Have you ever cashed in at the wrong moment?

882. Have you ever irked a postman?

Rich: Yes. You can find out all about it if you watch my *Oh Frig, I'm 50!* stand-up show.

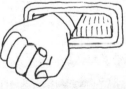

883. Is it legal for a man to marry his widow's sister?

Rich: If she loves him and wants to marry a dead body, then I say, 'Let the law be damned.' His death meant his marriage was over, so he's single.

884. What is the most annoying/pathetic trick question you have never encountered?

885. Can ghosts change clothes or do you have to stay in the clothes you died in? Why do you never see a naked ghost?

Rich: I presume there is a dressing room between life and death in which the nude are allowed to choose some clothing and the clothed are given the choice to change, then that's it. That's the only sensible explanation.

886. What one legal thing would you make illegal?

887. What one illegal thing would you make legal?

888. What is the most boring thing you can order in a café?

Rich: The man in the one I am in has just ordered a jacket potato with beans and cheese . . .
which is somehow more boring than one with just beans.

KATHERINE RYAN

What an amazing human being Katherine Ryan is! Fantastically funny and viciously caustic on stage, and wise and grounded in real life, she stands up for what she believes but also knows the value of getting on with things and thoroughly deserves her amazing success. Here are some questions inspired by her two appearances on the show:

889. Katherine has a cat called Sara Pascoe. Have you ever named a pet after a real person?

890. Katherine studied city planning at the University of Toronto. If you had to plan a new city, what would be the first five buildings you would insist were in it?

891. Katherine thinks that eating something whilst someone is trying to talk to you is a power move. Do you have a power move to ensure you get your own way?

892. As a child Katherine thought she would marry Adam Sandler. Who is the most reprehensible person you had a childhood crush on and how do you think it would have panned out if you had married them?

893. Katherine has never seen a Bigfoot despite being from Canada, but she has seen a bear, which is arguably not as impressive. Have you ever seen a bear?

894. If you could have a Willy Wonka-style golden ticket to go on a tour of any real factory in the world, which factory would you visit, and would you be disappointed if it wasn't gifted to you at the end?
Rich: The Ladybird book factory in Loughborough in 1972.

895. What's the best Venn diagram you've ever seen?

896. Have you ever used a cement mixer?
Rich: I think so. I helped actor Andrew Mackay lay his patio and we needed to mix cement, but maybe we did it in a bucket . . . I'm not sure now. It was a great day of manual labour for me, though. If only I could build physical things rather than wasting my life writing stupid questions.

897. Is social media a force for good or evil?

898. If someone from the eighties was brought forward in time to today and asked to guess what year they thought they were now in, what do you think their guess would be?

899. Would you rather suck off a troll or be bummed by a leprechaun?

NB The leprechaun has a much bigger and gnarlier penis than you might be expecting.

900. Who was the worst person who you were sad to hear had died?

Rich: For one second I was truly upset that Milwaukee Cannibal Jeffrey Dahmer had been murdered, and then I remembered he wasn't just a fun Hannibal Lecter fictional character but a real murderer. I guess a lot of people mourned Jimmy Savile before they found out the terrible and obvious truth about him too.

901. Is it better to have loved and lost than to have to eat nothing but Pop Tarts for a year?

902. Where did your family go on holiday when you were a child?

Rich: The Isle of Arran. I remember that it rained a lot, and we had a real fire. One time my dad let me sit on his knee and steer the car and I nearly drove us off the road. I was twenty-eight years old.

903. Do you think that the voice in your head that you perceive as yourself is the one making the actual decisions, or is there a shadowy 'other you' (for whom the 'you voice' is just a toadying spokesperson) who never speaks but makes all the actual choices that the 'you voice' then has to justify to you?

904. Would it be better to never be able to say 'yes' or never be able to say 'no'?

905. If you knew you couldn't be caught, would you cheat and steal? Or is it the chance that you could be caught that makes cheating and stealing fun? Or are you too afraid of being caught to ever cheat or steal?

906. If you had to have the head of another human being grafted on to your shoulders in order to save space and resources, whose head would you be okay with having placed next to yours? Would it be better or worse if it was your partner's? How much money would you have to be paid to go along with the arrangement? What if it was your head that was going to be put on someone else's body? Have a good think about it. It wouldn't all be bad.

907. Why don't we just have a worldwide referendum to determine which branch of religion is correct and then everyone has to accept that one? If there is a God, He or She would surely make sure the right branch of the right religion would win. Also, similar religions would have to join forces to be in with a chance of winning, which would iron out a lot of the superficial differences.

908. Do you think if the whole world believed in the same version of the same God that we'd just find other reasons to judge and murder each other?

909. What is the greatest misuse of time travel you have ever witnessed (probably in a TV show/film or book, but double points if it's from real life)?

Rich: It is the CBeebies TV show *Andy's Dinosaur Adventures*. Oh, you've broken a dinosaur egg in your museum – don't go back to Jurassic times to pick up a fresh one, just go back fifteen minutes and tell yourself to stop being such a clumsy prick ... and maybe get a job that doesn't involve you handling very fragile items every week. I hate Andy from *Andy's Dinosaur Adventures* and hope that he gets eaten by a dinosaur.

910. I call children 'sexcrement' as I view them as sexual excrement that you have failed to dispose of in a considerate manner. Have you ever created a cool new portmanteau word? If not, can you create one now? I will wait for you to Google 'portmanteau' if this question has not given you sufficient clues as to what it means.

911. What do you most miss about being a child? If you are a child, what do you think you'll miss about being a child when you are grown up?

912. What's the most surprising thing that you've ever found in a tumble dryer?

Rich: My cat Smithers liked to wee in ours, so probably cat urine.

913. How long can you go without checking your mobile phone?

914. Do you have a bucket list? That is, a list of all the different types of buckets that you hope to own before you die? How many of the buckets do you have so far?

915. You find out that science has been getting it wrong and there are actually 366 days in every year (367 in a leap year)! However, it's too much trouble to get the extra day added to the calendar so they're just going to plonk it at the end of the year, not name it or acknowledge it. No one has to work and no laws apply. Everyone will just pretend it isn't there. What do you do with the extra day?

916. What's the nicest true thing that you could say about me?

917. Question! How long do you think you could act like Destiny's Child and say 'Question!' before asking any question before you got bored or beaten up? Question! Why don't you try it?

Rich: Answer! Two times.

918. Have you ever been threatened with violence by Piers Morgan? Do you reckon you could take him if he came looking for a rumble?

Rich: I have and I do.

919. If you had to swap all the clothes you own with all the clothes of someone you know, whose clothes would you choose? Do you think they'd be as happy as you are to get to wear your clothes?

920. Who is your favourite David Copperfield: the Dickens character, the magician or the comedian from *Three of a Kind*? Or another David Copperfield, if you know one.

921. Have you ever worn a catsuit?

EMERGENCY QUESTIONS FOR THE MORAL LABYRINTH

Here are some real-life moral conundrums that Rich Herring has had to face. Most of them have to do with snacks that a fifty-year-old man has no business eating. He'll tell you what he ended up doing, but how would you act in the same situation? It's an Emergency Questions moral maze!

922. Rich was on a train and had paid extra money to sit in First Class so he could work. He was disappointed when he was charged for his meal, which he had thought would be free. Later, the refreshment trolley passed his seat and a big pack of overpriced Quavers fell off it without the lady noticing. Rich wasn't very hungry, but free food is free food and the evil train company charged a lot for the crisps. To keep them would be technically (and actually) theft and the loss might come out of the employee's wages. What would you do?

Rich: I kept the Quavers and ate them (quickly, in case I was caught, so I didn't enjoy them).

923. Rich was in a coffee shop with his infant daughter. He had bought a croissant and shared some of it with her, but she was still hungry. A stranger at the next table offered a Danish pastry from a crumpled paper bag. The Danish had not been bought at the café and also the man was a stranger who looked a bit destitute. However, he'd made this kind gesture with what might have been all he had to eat that day. Should Rich have accepted the gift and made his daughter eat the potentially poisoned cake out of a sense of liberal guilt, or refused the cake and upset the kind man who had offered it? Remember, Rich's wife would have been annoyed if the baby had been poisoned to death, but it would have been a shame to embarrass a nice, if slightly dirty, old man.

Rich: I accepted the Danish, and then broke off a tiny bit and gave it to my daughter. I left the rest of the Danish on the table – possibly the worst choice as the Danish would still have killed her if it were poisoned, and the man was probably offended by my wasting his precious food.

924. At an airport Rich passed a full bin with an open pornographic magazine on the top. A sad-eyed topless woman stared out amongst the rubbish. There were many reasons not to leave the magazine there.

a) It might be seen by a child, who should be protected from such images.

b) The magazine was in the regular bin when there were several recycling bins in the area.

c) As a gentleman I owed the young lady in the picture the dignity of not being displayed like this in a bin. The young ladies in this magazine had kindly posed nude for the masturbatory pleasure of gentlemen and to just throw them away was deeply disrespectful to them.

Would the polite thing for Rich to do be to discreetly take the magazine out of the bin and then later when alone masturbate fastidiously over every single image in it? Or, on the other hand, as it looked like fairly softcore porn of the kind that a teenage boy might enjoy but be unable to purchase, the magazine could be like manna from heaven for some lucky lad if he found it there. Should Rich deprive him of that treasure by removing it? Plus he is a nationally known comedian who doesn't want to be recognised by anyone and become nationally and internationally known as the Bin Porn Comedian – a man so desperate for masturbatory material that he would scavenge discarded, second-hand magazines. What would you do in these circumstances?

Rich: I left the magazine where it was, but only for fear of my spotless reputation being sullied. I then masturbated over hardcore pornography which is freely available online.

925. Rich was walking through Hitchin (in a bit of a distracted state because he'd just pocket-dialled someone and was trying to work out if he was ringing the person or the person was ringing him). He saw a group of people crouched on the pavement and noticed amongst them an old man, who looked okay but who Rich presumed had had a little turn and maybe had had to sit down or had fallen. As the man was surrounded by three or four people and in a potentially embarrassing situation, and Rich had no first-aid skills, he decided to move on and leave it to the people who had already stopped. Later, one of the people helping would angrily tweet that thirteen people had passed by and only comedian Richard Herring hadn't asked if everything was okay. Even though Rich explained that he hadn't seen what had happened but that the situation had appeared to be hand, and he didn't want to be a busybody hampering things with unnecessary questions that might embarrass the man, the tweeter insisted that Herring had looked down his nose at them. He hadn't, though. He'd merely looked at them. Was Rich right to walk on by? Or was he like the priest and the Levite in a modern-day version of The Good Samaritan?

Rich: I think the person who needs to question himself is the tweeter, who rather than assisting the fallen old man, was doing a survey of how many people were walking by, how they were responding and also making assumptions about what kind of face they were pulling. As you'll read elsewhere in this book, I once saved a falling nun, so my conscience is clear.

926. Rich was shopping at the supermarket. He was alone, but his wife and kids who were at soft play in town were going to meet him at the car later. However, they would not be coming into the supermarket with him. He decided that technically he was still allowed to park in one of the parking spaces for people with kids. I mean, the spirit of it is that they're there to help out people who are knackered from having to bring up the offspring they stupidly had, right? Was he correct?

927. Rich feels that pick 'n' mix sweets at service stations are outrageously overpriced. Therefore, as a civil rights protest akin to those of Martin Luther King, he always takes one free sweet every time he passes the display and eats it straight away without paying. Although this is technically (and actually) theft, he feels it is justified because the price that the service station is charging is technically (but not actually) a crime. He has never been caught and has probably ingested sweets worth hundreds of pounds (though their actual value is tens of pounds). Is what he is doing wrong?

Rich: I am like Robin Hood – stealing from the rich and giving to myself. Oh no, more like Ronnie Biggs, but less living in Brazil and more getting a slight sugar rush from those blue and red cola bottle sweets.

928. Rich was informed that a package had been delivered to his previous address. He went to pick it up and discovered that it was a big parcel of Marks & Spencer women's clothing. It was addressed to his wife but she hadn't ordered anything, and it actually turned out to be the purchases of a friend of hers who had previously sent a gift to their address and then inadvertently sent her own mail there. The friend had already received a replacement package of the same clothes after they hadn't arrived at her address. Should Rich return the clothing, keep it for his wife, sell it on eBay or give it to their friend so she has spare copies?

Rich: I elected to go to the nearest Marks & Spencer and queue up to return the package, but the cashier I gave it to didn't seem that impressed with my actions and said that most people wouldn't have bothered. Was I right to return it or just trying to make myself look good? And was I right to be disappointed that there was no reward from the shop for my honesty, or did that take all the positivity away?

929. Rich used to be a member of an overpriced gym in London. If you have seen him it will be of no surprise to you that he didn't often go, but he was still paying £85 a month to Ian Virgin (the owner) for the privilege of rarely visiting. After going swimming there once, Rich noticed that the dispenser for the bags to hold your wet swimming costume was open and that he could steal the big roll of bags and then use them to put cat litter in. This would be an inconvenience for any other gym user who wanted to put their damp swimming costume in a bag, but it would claw back a very few pence of the thousands of pounds that Rich had given to this institution. Was he justified in taking them?

930. Prior to performing at a festival in a field
in Kent, Rich had been assured by the organisers
of a free parking space to make his exit easier, as
he needed to drive a couple of hundred miles after
his afternoon set to do another gig in the evening.
On arrival, he found no parking space had been
reserved so he had to pay a tenner to park in the
regular car park. He explained to the attendant that
he was one of the acts, and the attendant said he
would refund him on the way out once he'd seen
his pass and told his supervisor to remember Rich.
On the way out, though, neither man was anywhere
to be seen and there was now a young woman at
the gate. Rich knew there was zero chance of her
having been told to refund him. She was arguing
with a drunk man away from the gate and had left
her money bag hanging on a fence post. Rich saw it
bulging with tenners and, realising the woman was
distracted, decided to retrieve his own ten pounds.
It was certainly a stupid risk that could have ended
with him leaving in a police car rather than heading
off to his next gig, but he got away with it and
the woman was perhaps lucky that he didn't take
the opportunity to help himself to a few hundred
pounds. Was this the right thing to do, however,
or should he just have let the tenner go? Or instead
asked for it back?

931. On holiday in Italy Rich and his wife had been coaxed into a restaurant, but then received very rude service from a disdainful waiter who seemed to be laughing at them. His wife wanted ravioli but the waiter told her that there was none left. This seemed unlikely in an Italian restaurant where they could surely make some, but they took him at his word. Later, they saw another table order ravioli and then receive it. The contemptuous service continued, and the food was bad. Rich put fifty euros in the bill wallet to pay for the meal before leaving, but when the wallet was returned there was still fifty euros in it. Rich's wife persuaded him to return the money to the till, but as he waited to do so the waiter was weird to him again and so he decided to walk out, meaning he had some bad pasta and a bottle of wine for free. Did the bad and mendacious service justify yet another food-based crime?

932. What is your favourite song by Aqua?
Rich: 'Turn Back Time'.

933. If you could travel back to medieval times, what single object would you take with you that would guarantee that you would be made king/ worshipped as a God?

934. Is honesty the best policy? If not, then what is the best policy?

935. By how many years after your death do you estimate that your existence will be totally forgotten?

936. What is your opinion of aubergines?

937. What was the last thing that you bleached?

938. What TV theme without lyrics do you always sing your own lyrics to?

Rich: On tour in the nineties, we watched *The X Files* on a video player on our tour bus. We always sang (in a high voice), '*The X Files* is on now' over and over again over the opening theme, and '*The X Files* is o-ver' over the end credits. I had a friend who would sing 'Bloody bugger, bloody bugger, bloody bugger, bloody hell' over the *Nationwide* theme tune.

939. Have you ever been watching an old video recorded off the telly and been discombobulated on seeing forgotten adverts, station idents or continuity announcers, like you've suddenly stepped into a different reality? What strange wonders have you seen?

940. What's the deepest puddle you've ever stepped in/walked through?

941. Have you ever been struck by how freaky lightning is?

942. Who is the best Benny?
Rich: The one from *Top Cat*.

943. If you could bring one vegetable to life – so it could walk around, have consciousness and emotions – which vegetable would you choose?

944. If you were turned into a ventriloquist dummy, would you secretly quite enjoy the experience?

945. Have you ever met someone called Ryan who is a reliable human being and not a love rat?
Rich: No, you haven't, even if you think you have. You are wrong. He was secretly awful.

946. Have you ever been in an open relationship, but the other person hadn't told you?

947. What is the best ice lolly?
Rich: It's the Fruit Pastille lolly.
No argument allowed.

948. Do you think you've already had over half the orgasms that you're ever going to have?

949. What's the most impressive thing that you've ever been underneath?

950. When you are dead, would you prefer your body to be interred in a huge pyramid built in the centre of your hometown along with many riches and all your living slaves, or be put in a bin liner and thrown illegally into a skip?

951. If the sun wasn't going to come up tomorrow unless you threw a member of your family into a volcano, which member of your family would you throw into the volcano? Or would you not throw anyone in and doom your hemisphere to icy death?

952. Have you ever been able to listen to someone talking about Uranus, without at least thinking 'your anus'?

Rich: Not once. Even if they try to get around it by saying 'Urr-an-us', that just doubly makes me think 'your anus', because I know they are trying to avoid saying 'your anus'.

953. Have you ever been to Aldershot?

Rich: I am there right now. How funny you should ask! The people who live here are not happy, but they're not as unhappy as they should be.

954. What's your favourite flap?

955. What's with all the salted caramel? What disgusting thing would you add to a delicious thing to create a somehow delicious thing?

956. What's the best weed?

957. Have you ever had an out-of-body experience? Have you ever really had an in-body experience? Or do you live your whole life feeling you are outside of yourself, watching this idiot make the same mistakes over and over, unable to do anything to stop them?

958. Do you have any ambition to be the Thane of Cawdor?

959. Would you like to have lived in Ancient Rome? What if you didn't get to choose which class of citizen you were? Would you take the chance?

Rich: I would so like to see Rome in its pomp that I would take the spin of the wheel, and if I ended up as a slave being bummed by Caecilius then so be it.

960. What (or who) would you like to see in its pomp?

Rich: I'd prefer to see Pompeii in its pomp because the repetition of 'pomp' is more satisfying. Also, that's where Caecilius lived, so he wouldn't have to travel so far to bum me.

961. If you had to be bummed by an Ancient Roman (or an ancient Roman) – if you *had* to be – which Roman would you choose to bum you?

962. Would you prefer to be Mike Reid or Mike Read? NB Mike Reid is the comedian and *EastEnders* actor. Mike Read is the calypso-singing DJ and manager of *Saturday Superstore*.

963. If there was a TV show called *My Creed*, would you be more likely to watch it if it was hosted by Mike Reid (assuming he hadn't died) or Mike Read (assuming he was allowed back on TV after all the unpleasantness)?

964. Do you have an envelope cupboard?

965. How good are you at wrapping presents? *Rich:* Fucking useless. I like your presents to come in a crumpled ball.

966. Have you ever had a crumpled ball?

967. To beard or not to beard?

968. Do you lie to your dentist about how often you brush your teeth and/or to your doctor about how much you drink?

969. Do you have a switch in your house that apparently does nothing? Do you fear that it actually does something? What do you fear it might do?

970. What's the best town ending in 'ford'?
Rich: If this comes up on *Pointless*, I am saying Bishop's Stortford.

971. Would you be screwed if the Internet stopped working? Could you cope if it went down for an hour? A day? A week? For ever?

972. Have you ever picked up a randomly ringing phone in a public phone box? Who was on the other end?

Rich: I did. In Weston-super-Mare in about 1982. There was a lonely-sounding woman on the end who wanted to know about me and mildly propositioned me. I was still five years away from losing my virginity and hung up. It's a shame for that woman that the Internet didn't exist then, but maybe ringing phone boxes and hoping for the best occasionally worked.

973. If you were only allowed to have twelve bones in your body (and no kind of implants to substitute for others), which twelve of your bones would you elect to keep?

974. If you had to be locked in a room with three presenters of *Top of the Pops* from the seventies (still alive and as active as they were in that period) for 24 hours – if you *had* to be – which three would you be locked in the room with?

Rich: What's interesting here is if you try to think of three you'd be safe with, or three you reckon you could take down in a three on one fight. There are some other options too. Personally, I'd go for the safe triumvirate of David 'Kid' Jenson, Peter Powell and Andy Peebles (who presented once on 11 October 1979).

975. Have you ever been a gooseberry?

976. Would you rather be He-Man or Skeletor? Like Milton's Satan, do you feel that Skeletor's persistence in the face of constant and inevitable defeat is actually quite admirable? But with the additional disability that he is literally just a skeleton? In a sense, does he not represent all of us when faced with muscle-bound bullies? Discuss.

BOB MORTIMER

It's hard to pick a favourite podcast from the huge number that have been made, but if I had to, I would probably plump for one with Bob Mortimer. He is the most naturally and effortlessly funny man and incredibly charming. I have just realised that I am in love with him.

977. Bob Mortimer comes from Linthorpe in Middlesbrough, just a quarter of a mile from Rich's grandparents' house (and Chris Rea possibly lived in their street), and the pair were able to reminisce about specific roads and shops. What celebrity lives nearest to the home of your grandparents?

978. Rich talked about visiting his grandparents' houses years after they had died and finding the places looked quite different to his memories of them. Have you experienced the haunting feeling of revisiting once very familiar houses and finding them strangely unfamiliar?

979. Bob fought and beat Les Dennis in a celebrity boxing match. Who is the least offensive person that you have punched?

980. Bob fought Darren Day in a celebrity boxing match. Who is the most offensive person that you have punched?

981. As we discussed dishwashers and other kitchen appliances, Bob asked his own pertinent question: Do you believe in Calgon? Have you ever had an appliance break down due to limescale build-up that Calgon would have sorted out? Rich wondered if the cost of all the Calgon over the lifetime of an appliance would add up to more than the cost of a new machine. What do you think?

982. If you could remember your birth and infancy, do you think it would cloud your opinion of your parents?

983. Do you correct people's grammar and spelling on social media or is it a bigger sin to point out such mistakes than it is to make them? What has been the most annoying error that you have corrected or have resisted correcting?

Rich: Today, in a thread about John Noakes, in which his name is correctly spelled, one person is persistently calling him 'Knowksey'. It's driving me insane. But I would never be the kind of dick who would correct someone in this situation. Instead, I am going to passive-aggressively write about it in a book, which will be read by far more people, and hopefully that person will see this and feel the shame they should be feeling. If any grammatical errors have slipped through in this book, do not contact me or the publisher, but please write your own book in which you include corrections of my mistakes. I mean, come on! 'Knowksey'?

984. **What would it take for you to fellate the actor Keith Allen?**

Rich: I am hoping I can have my arch-enemy Keith Allen on the podcast one day simply so I can ask him: 'What would it take for you to suck your own cock?'

985. **Have you ever been called a nickname that you didn't like?**

Rich: When they tell you what it is, then call them that for the rest of your life, or their life, whichever is longer.

986. **If a tree falls in the forest and no one is around to see it, does it use its branches like arms to lessen the impact of the fall?**

987. **What's so great about being meek? Is inheritance of the earth really a just reward for not getting in anyone's way?**

988. Given that bears don't exclusively shit in the woods and polar bears basically never do, what do you think people mean when they say 'Do bears shit in the woods?' Sometimes? Not always? No, if you're talking about polar bears?

989. Is the Pope Catholic?

Rich: Most people say 'yes' to this one, but I hope it will lead many of you to a long conversation about Christian doctrine and how Catholicism has changed over the centuries. He is, though. He's one of the main ones.

990. Is Jesus Catholic?

Rich: This should lead to more arguments . . . but He's definitely Jewish. Or He was last time He showed up.

991. Have you ever had an internal battle? Who won?

992. Would you rather be the best at what you do but no one has ever heard of you, or world famous for being the best at what you do but actually terrible at it?

993. Do you think towns should bring back the forum?

994. Did you know that Jools Holland's *Hootenanny* is pre-recorded? What do you think about that? What do you think Jools Holland does on the real New Year's Eve? He can't go out, lest his deception is discovered.

Rich: I did know, because I was invited on a couple of occasions in the early 2000s, and in one of those years I spent the real New Year's Eve on my own, sadly watching myself having a great time surrounded by celebrities on TV. Could there be a more poignant example of the falsity of show business?

995. Do you think smokers have a (possibly unfair) advantage when it comes to being on the pull?

Rich: Yes, especially now you have to go outside of pubs to smoke. I was once cuckolded by a smoker who snogged the girl I was on a date with as they were standing around outside. Also, you can ask people for a light to cheat your way into a conversation. Also, you are clearly much cooler than a non-smoker. True, they will live longer, but it's just longer to be on their own.

996. Have you ever taken part in an identity parade – either trying to pick out the criminal, being one of the people who isn't a criminal or being the alleged criminal?

Rich: I was once asked to be one of the guys who might be the criminal. I wasn't the criminal, but the woman who looked at us chose the wrong guy. We all laughed about how he'd have to go to prison now.

SHUT UP!

Here are four questions to help you end a conversation (to be fair, a few of the previous 996 questions might do that too, but these are designed to bring a chat to an end):

997. Do you think women should be treated as if they are equal?

998. Do you want to talk about Brexit?

999. Can I please tell you in huge detail about my religious beliefs on the condition that you don't question or contradict me?

1000. Shall we go to bed now? Not with each other ... unless that's what you want?

EMERGENCY QUESTION 1001

1001. Have you used Emergency Questions in any remarkable or unusual real-life situation?
Answer from Rich's Twitter page: Johnnie Blott –
I win this! Trapped in the Himalayas for a week after an earthquake waiting for a helicopter to rescue us.
#lifesavingEQs

BONUS QUESTIONS

1. What was the weirdest reason you ever skived off school?

2. If you only had a week to live, who would you tell to go fuck themselves?

3. If your genitals had to be replaced by the face of one of the Muppets (the face would be able to interact and communicate in exactly the same way as the puppet), which Muppet face would replace your genitals? Please explain your thinking.

4. What's the furthest you've driven in one day? Did anything remarkable happen on that drive?

5. What would it take for you to teabag Jacob Rees-Mogg?

6. Do you favour the death penalty for people who say 'expresso' instead of 'espresso'? If not, what would be your pacific punishment for such a crime?

7. What is your longest-running petty disagreement with a friend or relation?

8. If you could burn one building to the ground without harming anyone or being prosecuted for arson, which edifice would you torch?

9. Would you prefer to have odourless farts or self-cleaning teeth?

10. If you had to be given oral sex by a dinosaur – if you *had* to be – which dinosaur would you like to be mouthed to completion by?

11. Richard accidentally elbowed Denise van Outen in the face on Channel 5's *Celebrity Game Night*. What is the worst injury you have directly or indirectly caused to a celebrity or person of renown? The worst injury to the most famous person scores the most points.

12. Do you think you'd make a good Pope?

13. What item belonging to your neighbour do you covet the most?

14. Have you ever colluded with a Russian?

15. Have you ever canoodled with a Russian?

16. Have you ever canoed with a Russian?

17. Do you think they should introduce VAR (video assisted referee) technology for everyday life? What incidents or arguments would you want replayed and resolved from today?

18. What extra item would you add to the game Rock, Paper, Scissors to liven things up and what would it beat and be defeated by?

19. Who did you last wave your bare bum at?

20. Have you ever attempted to create a monument that will stand for millennia? How did you get on?

21. What's the most unlikely thing you've ever seen up a mountain?

22. Richard has been meaning to clean up the drain outside his kitchen ever since he moved two years ago. What is the longest running chore that you've been intending to do, but keep putting off?

23. What was the worst thing a teacher ever said or did to you at school? And was it a games teacher?

24. What's the most surprising thing you've seen going on in someone's house or garden when you've been sitting on a passing train or bus?

25. On a scale of 1–13 where 1 is very dirty and 13 is very clean, how clean are your windows?

CELEBRITY ANSWERS TO EMERGENCY QUESTIONS

Here are a handful of my favourite answers from guests on the *RHLSTP* podcast.

If you had to have sex with an animal – if you *had* to – which animal would you have sex with and why?
David Mitchell: What if I just swatted a fly with my cock? Would that count? Maybe a medium-sized drugged animal – a very calm elderly Labrador.

Does sex with a robot count as cheating on your partner?
David Mitchell: I don't think my wife would mind me having sex with a robot that looked like C-3PO.

If you had to go on holiday with a *Spitting Image* puppet – bearing in mind that the puppet would choose the destination and you'd be accompanied by the puppeteer and voiceover artist, who would only be able to interact with you in character via the puppet – which puppet would you choose?

David Mitchell: Melvyn Bragg. He'd choose a nice destination. The showy choice would be some member of the Thatcher cabinet – the screeching Douglas Hurd puppet. But I think that would be wearing. And I wouldn't be going on this holiday for anecdotal value, I'd like to have a nice, relaxed time. If not the Melvyn Bragg puppet then one of the general members of the public. Puppets that weren't a specific celebrity. Because I imagine whoever did the voices for that would be grateful for the holiday.

Would you prefer to have a hand made out of ham or an armpit that dispensed sun cream?

Adam Buxton: I'd like a ham hand. I like ham. My mum's South American so I'm dark skinned anyway. I don't really need the sun cream. To me, protecting myself from the sun is less important than supplying my face with ham.

What do you most regret destroying with fire?

Richard Osman: I'd have to say, Windsor Castle.

If you had to be anally violated by a popular chocolate bar – if you *had* to – which bar would you like inserted in your anus?

Richard Osman: I guess, a Drifter? I'm trying to think of something that's narrow but would have some structural integrity. You know what I mean?

Have you ever seen a Bigfoot?

Dawn French: I've seen a big foot. I *was* married to Lenny Henry.

Would you rather be lactose intolerant or Prime Minister of the Central African Republic?

Ed Miliband: I'd rather be the Prime Minister of the Central African Republic, obviously. How is that even a question?

Would you rather be the face of a twin (mostly) absorbed in utero, staring out of the stomach of your otherwise regular twin (you would be able to think independently and talk and pass comment on what they were up to and chat with them if they're lonely or if you're lonely) or be the prisoner of a randy Bigfoot, who so far has treated you kindly enough but has a look in its eye?

Greg Davies: So, distilling those down a bit? Oh, so I'm just a small face within someone else's stomach. Would I rather be that or would I rather risk being potentially fucked by a sasquatch? Well, Richard, in answer to your question, I would, I think, I would prefer the freedom of moving around and fending for myself and the small chance that the Bigfoot wouldn't fuck me than being absorbed within someone else's stomach. So I think that would be my answer, yeah.

Have you ever seen a ghost?

Mackenzie Crook: I pretended I saw one for quite a few years. For quite a few, when I was a teenager . . . it was a sleepover at a friend's house, at a vicarage. Sort of a prime location for a ghost. I think I saw something out of the corner of my eye, looked around, it was nothing. I thought, I might just pretend I saw a ghost. And I kept it up for quite a few years. It was a bloke with a tray – a butler, an old butler.

Have you ever been brass rubbing?

Sara Pascoe: Brass rubbing. The London Brass Rubbing Centre is actually right next to Charing Cross Station at St. Martin-in-the-Fields Church, which is the Royal Family's parish church, which is where Prince Charles was christened. They also do tai chi just outside. They changed one of their stained-glass windows to make it less secular and put a moon up there, which is really beautiful. And no, I've never been brass rubbing.

If you had a finger that could cure rectal cancer, but only if you pushed it hard up the anus of the cancer sufferer, would you cure anyone, everyone, or be like Jesus and just cure a few?

Limmy: Um, just the sort of good people ... like, say, people I didn't agree with politically, I would let them die. People I didn't like, or anybody who maybe wronged me in Primary 1 or something like that. See them on Facebook, talking about how, you know, terrible news and all that. I'd say, 'Listen, I've got this ability'. And then go, 'Wait a fucking minute, I remember you. Bye.' I would use it for evil rather than good.

Where do you get your crazy ideas from?

Sarah Millican: What, like coming on this podcast?

ACKNOWLEDGEMENTS

Thanks to Chris Evans (not that one), Ben Walker, all the podcast crew, but especially my favourite Human Centipede George, Craig and Kinga, Martin and everyone at the Leicester Square Theatre, James Taylor (not that one), Katie McKay and everyone at Avalon, Adam Strange, Hannah Boursnell and the brilliant team at Sphere, all the guests from the podcast particularly those who feature in the book and all the badgers and dripsters who keep the podcasts going. Love and thanks to my wife Catie and our sexcrement, Phoebe and Ernie.

Song lyric credits: 'Do You Know The Way To San Jose?' by Burt Bacharach and Hal David © Burt Bacharach; 'Have A Cracking Christmas' by Woolworths; 'Learn To Live With What You Are' by Ben Folds © Universal Music; 'Swinging On A Star' by Jimmy Van Heusen and Johnny Burke © Bourne Company & Dorsey Brothers Music, Inc.; 'Three Times A Lady' by Lionel Richie © Motown Record Company, L.P. and 'War' words and music by Norman Whitfield, Barrett Strong, Dana R. Scott, Pete Peterson and James R. Thomas © Aroun' Town Prod., Inc.